ORLANDO WEST SOWETO

ORLANDO WEST SOWETO

AN ILLUSTRATED HISTORY

NOOR NIEFTAGODIEN AND SALLY GAULE

WITS UNIVERSITY PRESS

Published in South Africa by:

Wits University Press
1 Jan Smuts Avenue
Johannesburg
www.witspress.co.za

First published 2012

ISBN 978-1-86814-544-7 (Print)
ISBN 978-1-86814-595-9 (Digital)

Edited by Monica Seeber
Cover design and layout by Hothouse South Africa
Printed and bound by Creda Communications

CONTENTS

FOREWORD

One of the tragedies of apartheid was the marginalisation of the history of the black majority of this country. Since at least the 1980s the project to recover this history, which was then called 'People's History', and which was driven by anti-apartheid activists and radical historians, has made great strides in redressing the imbalances of past historical accounts. The re-writing of history has gathered momentum since the advent of democracy and a considerable body of literature has been published about the key figures in the liberation struggle as well as the main events that contributed to overthrowing apartheid. And yet so much more needs to be done to uncover the hidden stories of our communities.

It is in this context that *Orlando West, Soweto,* an oral history documentation of the joys and struggles of the Orlando community should be understood. Orlando West is renowned for its historic contributions to the liberation of our people. It is here on 16 June 1976 where thousands of students shouted with one voice: 'To hell with Afrikaans' and 'Down with apartheid'. Their courage and determination heralded the beginning of the end of minority rule.

Orlando West, and in particular Vilakazi Street, is the known home of two Nobel Peace Prize winners, the former state president, Nelson Mandela, and Archbishop Emeritus Desmond Tutu. Orlando East is associated with the Sofasonke Party and is home to its founder, James Mpanza, the first man to own horses in the township. Orlando is indeed the home of the struggle and, perhaps, can even be referred to as the 'political' home of South Africa and the bedrock of our nation's march towards freedom.

The township of Orlando (the area now known as Orlando East) was established in 1932 as one of the first township settlements developed to house the increasing number of African migrant workers drawn to the burgeoning mining camp of Johannesburg. In 1937 , not long after the establishment of Orlando, a group of young soccer players formed what has become one of South Africa's biggest soccer teams of all time, Orlando Pirates.

In its eighty years of existence, Orlando has represented an evolving kaleidoscope of South Africa's modern history. This book is the story of the people of Orlando, and is told largely through their accounts. It is a recollection of fond and of painful memories.

This book demonstrates the commitment of the City of Johannesburg Metropolitan Municipality to contribute to the important task of uncovering the history of our communities and we hope this will be the start of a trend that explores communities' histories through their people.

Councillor Ruby Mathang

Member of Mayoral Committee:
Development Planning and Urban Management

City of Johannesburg
20 April 2012

ACKNOWLEDGEMENTS

The proposal to undertake a history project in Orlando West was raised at a community meeting of the Vilakazi Street Precinct Upgrade Project. It was an interesting idea, considering the area has received considerable attention due to its centrality in the 1976 student uprising and being home to two Nobel Peace Laureates, Nelson Mandela and Desmond Tutu. Research conducted on the iconic event and on these leaders has illuminated some aspects, especially the politics, on Orlando's history. Nonetheless, residents expressed the view that the rich and diverse histories of the local community had not received adequate attention. The Johannesburg Development Agency (JDA) was therefore mandated by the community to include an oral history of the area in its project plans. In 2009 the History Workshop (University of the Witwatersrand) commenced with this work and after consultation agreed on a number of modest objectives, which included recording life histories of between thirty and forty residents and undertaking archival research, producing a documentary based on the interviews and photographing various aspects of everyday life in the area. In addition local researchers were to be trained and a manuscript written. The achievement of these objectives is due to the support and contributions from numerous people.

The JDA not only provided funds but offered all sorts of logistical support and advice. Kirsten Harrison and Tanya Zack embraced the community's proposal with enthusiasm and were the early drivers behind the project. Their insistence on proper historical research was crucial in defining its character. Thanduxolo Ntoyi played a critical role as the liaison between our work as researchers, the JDA and the community. Thando Mendrew, the current CEO of the JDA, and Susan Monyai were exceedingly helpful and were critical in steering the project to its conclusion in the form of this book.

Ali Hlongwane played an important role in facilitating relations with the existing heritage organisations. The Hector Pieterson Museum, Mandela Museum and the June 16th Foundation supported and encouraged our work. The former also hosted our workshop with teachers. Several other local entities and people, including the Ward Committee, local councillors and political activists engaged us throughout the life of the project. Sifiso

Ndlovu, the key historian on the Soweto Uprising, was always generous in his response to our queries.

Dumisane Khesa, Sakhile Mthabela and Tshepo Ramutumbu were the main local researchers on the project. Two others, Joy Matthews and Boitumelo Khoza left when they found long-term employment elsewhere. The remaining three attended training workshops, conducted interviews and spent many weeks in the archives. Despite some challenges their collective effort added value to the research. It was agreed at the outset to photograph contemporary life in the area and to collect photos from residents. Sally Gaule brought her skills and experience to bear on both these aspects and mentored Sakhile in the process. The two of them mounted a successful exhibition based on the photographs taken during the course of the project. In addition, Sally has produced an insightful and sensitive photo-essay as the last chapter of the book.

Wonderboy Peters and his crew of young film-makers spent a number of weekends video-recording interviews with several residents, and produced a documentary on the history of Orlando, which has been enthusiastically received in the community. Copies have been distributed to interviewees and schools in the area.

The research team based at the History Workshop was, as usual, outstanding. Tshepo Moloi played a pivotal role in conducting interviews and acting as a mentor to the local researchers. His expertise as an interviewer is evident in the documentary and this book. Transcribing interviews is a critical but often neglected part of oral history. Plantinah Dire, Tshegofatso Leeuw, Sibongile Mgwebi, Reabetswe Kgaruwe, Mojabeng Liholo, Bongani Khumalo and Musawenkosi Malabela ensured the interviews were reliably transcribed and translated. Our administrators, Zahn Gowar, Gugulethu Nyathikazi and Ms Sifiso Ndlovu often went beyond the call of duty to address a steady stream of demands. Phil Bonner was always supportive and participated in the training workshop.

The librarians and archivists at the university's William Cullen Library were very helpful and exceedingly patient in assisting our local researchers. Without the support of Wits Press this book would not have seen the light of day. Monica Seeber was a patient and professional editor, and Melanie Pequeux steered the project to its conclusion.

Many residents of Orlando West welcomed us into their homes to be interviewed and photographed. Their stories are at the heart of this book. We hope our various efforts have met their expectations of contributing to an understanding of the rich history of the area.

Noor Nieftagodien

History Workshop
University of the Witwatersrand

LIST OF INTERVIEWEES

Lungiswa Bacela
Toto Davashe
Alfred Jacobs
Mogari Khomo
Ntombi Khumalo
Setshebi Kota
Sechaba Lepote
Patrick Madibe
Grace Kekeletso Mafafane
Mary Makola
Mirriam Mankula
Rebecca Matthews
Sonnyboy Matthews
Ndukuzakhe Isaac Mazibuko
Ntlantla Daniel Mazibuko
Mbulelo Mbele
Rev. Lulama Walter Mbete
Zamo Mbutho
Peter Mkhasibe
Reverend Ishmael Papi Morris
Tseko Mothopeng
Ms. Motopanyane
Shadrack Mutau
China Ngema and Mrs Masoma
Enoch Nhlapho
Collin Nxumalo
Eric Osiba
Nukuthula Cynthia Ramoitheki
Sidney Ramokgopa
Patrick Sekuthe
Andronica Bahedile Sithole
Mr Sithole and Mrs Sithole
Rita Tandy
Wilfred Boy Thabethe
Shirley Thathi
Elizabeth Nonki Tsimo
Catherine Vilakazi
Jacky Vilakazi
Mzwakhe Washington Sixolo
Mrs Sixolo
Thami Zitha

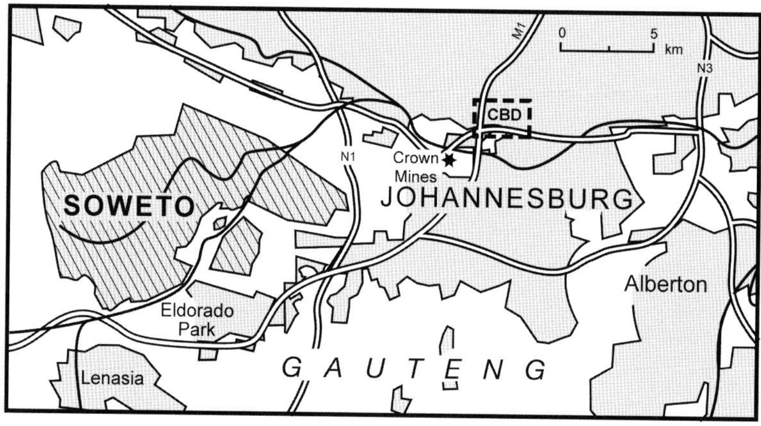

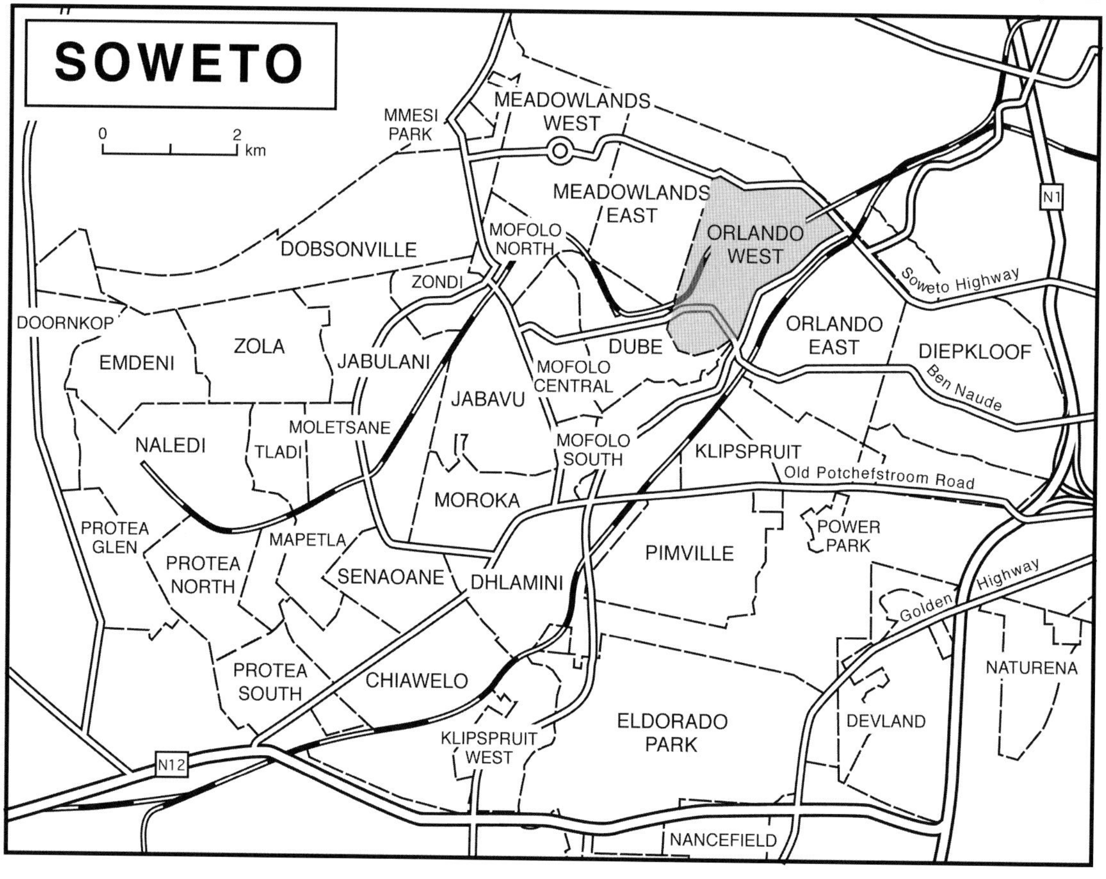

Map by Wendy Job

CHAPTER ONE

ORIGINS

SOWETO AND JOHANNESBURG, INEXTRICABLY LINKED. THEIR SEPARATE histories cast light on each other.

Formally established in 1886 after the discovery of gold, Johannesburg grew rapidly over the next couple of decades to become South Africa's main economic centre and its most populous city. In 1887, the mining town set up to accommodate early mine diggers contained a mere 3 000 souls, but as the gold rush gathered momentum its population exploded. Immigrants poured in – from the region and from all over the world. By 1899 there were 100 000 people in Johannesburg. And in 1911, only a quarter of a century after the founding of the city, there were about 240 000. Johannesburg's rate of growth was exceeded only by New York's.

The name Soweto was only adopted in 1963, after the rapid expansion of townships in the south-western areas of Johannesburg from the 1950s. Before then, the city's non-mining African people, like many other poor inhabitants of this rapidly expanding 'city of gold', were to be found in the inner city slums and municipal locations. But the origins of Soweto go back to the turn of the twentieth century. There were three pivotal moments in the pre-apartheid development of the township: the 1904 plague, the establishment of Orlando in 1930, and Mpanza's squatter movement of the mid 1940s. Each of these contributed in its own way to making Soweto the pre-eminent location of Johannesburg's African population.

At the end of the Anglo-Boer War, the newly appointed engineer of Johannesburg, Major WAJ O'Meara, expressed outrage over the slumyards

Source: Wits Historical Papers

LEFT: Early Johannesburg, 1886–1888

CENTRE: Johannesburg, c1900?

RIGHT: Johannesburg, 1911

in the north-west of the city. There was no public housing, and Burghersdorp, Brickfields, Fordsburg, 'Kaffir Location' and 'Coolie Location' had become the main residential sites for the city's poor working class. It was 'Coolie Location' that most angered city officials, not only because they saw it as a risk to the health of the town, but also because Indian traders living in the location were perceived as a threat to white small businesses. Writing recently about the contestations that preceded the early founding of what was to become Soweto, the medical historian Howard Phillips has explained that the city authorities proposed to deal with these 'problems' by an improvement scheme, the primary aim of which was to re-order 'the racial, social and sanitary geography of a key part of Johannesburg, which it now damningly labelled "the insanitary area".' A commission established to consider the future of this area proposed the destruction of the location and removal of its inhabitants to racially segregated areas.

The Public Health Committee was appalled that 'the Malays, Indians and Kaffirs were jumbled all over the place … [alongside] men and women of various colours and nationalities'. What the planners, engineers and doctors who ran the committee aspired to, argues Phillips, was 'a modern, ordered city, with its population clearly sorted by race, class and ethnicity once and for all.' Johannesburg was to be properly segregated for the benefit of its white population. 'The existence and future of Johannesburg as a white man's town in a white man's country,' stated the committee, 'is, in our opinion, involved … [as] the proper development of the European population would be endangered by the present state of things.'

Source: Wits Historical Papers

Source: Wits Historical Papers

The opportunity to realise this vision of the city, a white man's town in a white man's country, arose in March 1904 with the outbreak of pneumonic plague in 'Coolie Location'. Indian and African residents were blamed, and although none of the more than one thousand African residents of the location succumbed to the disease (it was probably imported from outside the country), the authorities moved swiftly to destroy the slum. On 20 March, a police cordon surrounded the location to prevent anyone from entering or leaving. Plans were then implemented to move the residents to a quarantined site, and finally 'Coolie Location' was demolished by fire. All of this took place in a matter of days.

The authorities wanted to move coloureds and Indians to an area around Fordsburg and Mayfair, but strident objections from white residents thwarted that plan and so it was decided to move all 'Coolie Location's' population to Klipspruit Farm, about twelve miles from the city. Klipspruit Farm's main connection to the city had been as the proposed site of a sewage farm. The city, though, owned the Klipspruit, and the main railway line ran past it. In September 1904, the Johannesburg Council decided to declare Klipspruit a permanent settlement for the city's African population – or at least for those not living in compounds or in backrooms on their employers' properties. In 1906, residents of 'Kaffir Location' were moved to Klipspruit. By 1908, the number of African people in the new location stood at 2 500. Indians were relocated to 'Malay Location', which was situated near the old 'Coolie Location'.

The primary objective behind this early urban segregation project was succinctly captured by the Public Health Committee: 'The advantages of keeping the native quarters completely away from the white population will be obvious to everyone, whether one considers the interests of the native or those of the poorer class of Europeans.' Keeping the 'races' apart was supposedly desirable for everyone, but especially for poor whites who tended to live and mix with poor blacks in the urban slums.

But despite this removal scheme only a small percentage of the city's African population not residing in compounds was relocated to Klipspruit. The rest continued to live in and around the city and, after the formation of Union in 1910, which united the British colonies of the Cape and Natal with the Afrikaaner Republics of the Free State and Transvaal into a single country, they also set up homes in freehold and municipal locations.

Johannesburg's African population after the First World War was in the region of 105 000 persons, nearly half of them working on the mines and accommodated in prison-like compounds. A further 30 000 were domestic workers who lived on the premises of their employers, and a mere 4 000 lived in municipal locations such as Klipspruit. Then there were a further estimated 17 000 Africans crammed into the insalubrious slums dotted across the city. The discrepancy between the populations of the official municipal locations and the slums reflected both the tardiness in the state's provision of formal housing to urban Africans, and the preference of people to live close to the city.

In the post-war period there was a continued influx into the urban areas and, in the absence of housing, more and more people were forced to settle in the already overcrowded slums. By 1927 the overall population of these settlements had increased to 40 000. It was this steadily growing urban African working class, desperately struggling to establish roots in the city, that caused consternation for the authorities. From the perspective of the state, slums were sites of all sorts of antisocial behaviour, including oppositional politics. Its response was to plan for the systematic elimination of the slums, and to move Africans to better controlled municipal locations.

Until the end of the First World War, urban growth proceeded unevenly and haphazardly, and the authorities tended to respond to urban crises in an *ad hoc* way, as they happened. But under the impact of a wave of militant struggles by black workers, and in the context of the devastating impact of the 1918 influenza epidemic, the state was spurred into more decisive action. Some town planners attempted to import the notion of the 'garden city' which would provide more public direction over the mainly uncontrolled private development that characterised urban life in the early part of the century. Above all, the state was determined to better manage the movement of Africans into the urban areas and to place them in properly controlled locations when they settled in the cities.

Source: Wits Historical Papers

Inner city slum removals

Prospect Location, 1937

Source: Wits Historical Papers

The promulgation of the Native (Urban) Areas Act of 1923 was intended to meet these objectives. The Act was a hybrid piece of legislation. On the one hand, it espoused the principles enunciated by the Stallard Commission of 1922, which had infamously declared that an African 'should only be allowed into the urban areas, which are essentially the white man's creation, when he is willing to enter and minister to the needs of the white man, and should depart therefrom when he ceases so to minister'. On the other hand, when it empowered local authorities to set aside land for black residential purposes it recognised the need to create conditions for the settlement of an urban African population in order to provide a reliable supply of labour to secondary industry.

The growing demand for housing and the desire to eliminate slums led the government to establish Orlando (named after the chairman of the Native Affairs Committee, Edwin Orlando Leake) in the early 1930s. The promulgation of the Slums Act in 1934 gave the government the legislative muscle to act decisively against urban slums, with the result that thousands of African families were evicted from areas in and around the city centre. For example, in the late 1930s approximately 7 000 African residents of Prospect Township on the south-eastern outskirts of Johannesburg's central business district, were removed and offered accommodation in Orlando.

When the original Orlando (Orlando East) was established in 1931, the authorities described it as a 'model native township' that was supposedly planned along the lines of a garden city. The new location, it promised, would be characterised by tree-lined streets, business opportunities and recreation facilities. So impressed were town planners with this new scheme that the plans for Orlando won a town-planning competition. Reflecting the views of a somewhat conservative section of the African urban elite, the popular African newspaper *Bantu World,* predicted on 14 May 1932 that the new township 'will undoubtedly be somewhat of a paradise [that] will enhance the status of the Bantu within the ambit of progress and civilisation.'

In reality, the new municipal location was only a 'model township' from the perspective of the authorities. It fell far short of providing its residents with even the basic amenities required for decent living. In the book *Soweto – A History*, Nelson Botile, a resident of Orlando, vividly described the condition of the house his family moved into:

> The walls were not plastered, they were rough and the floor was just grass. It was not cemented. My father started plastering the house once we were inside. The houses had no taps. We didn't have sewerage – we had what was called the bucket system and we had these people coming at night to remove the sanitation. The streets were not tarred and they had no names. The houses only had numbers.

Source: Wits Historical Papers

New housing in Orlando

The low standard of housing erected in Orlando prefigured the massive housing development in 'model townships' under apartheid. In his 2004 work *Johannesburg: The Making and Shaping of the City*, the urban geographer Keith Beavon describes the township that emerged to the south west of Johannesburg after 1940 as 'a large, sprawling urbanised area without true urban amenities. It was threaded through by dusty, unpaved roads along which were erected monotonous ranks of identical, small, temporary, single storey "matchbox" houses (predominantly between 40m^2 and 44m^2 in size) lit by candles and oil lamps, where cooking was done on paraffin and coal stoves. All but the barest of daily necessities had to be bought in Johannesburg and carted back on the inadequate public transport system from the white city.'

In the mid-1930s, the authorities may have imagined that they had achieved a degree of control over the lives of urban Africans: slums were successfully being eliminated and municipal locations appeared to be functioning relatively well. Although the African population of Johannesburg continued to grow, the rate of increase was rather modest and at the start of the Second World War the number of African people living in locations had increased to just over 100 000 (importantly from the perspective of the authorities, nearly half of this number, according to Beavon, lived in Pimville and Orlando). But these official figures obscured the profound transformation that was already under way in the country's urban areas.

From the late 1930s, South Africa underwent a massive economic transformation that was spurred on by the Second World War. By the end of the war secondary industry had eclipsed mining as the main contributor to the national economy. In the decade from 1936 to 1946, the number of factories in the country grew by nearly fifty per cent, creating an unprecedented demand for labour, especially cheap African labour. Consequently, the influx of Africans to the urban areas grew fast during this time. It was also spurred on by growing impoverishment in the rural areas. From the late 1930s, there was a critical shift in the profile of Africans living in urban areas: between 1936 and 1946 the African urban population increased from just over a million to nearly two million. And, critically, the number of African women in the urban areas rose from about 350 000 to about 650 000 during the same period.

Paradoxically, the state's programme of housing delivery for Africans that followed slum clearance in the early to mid-1930s was rapidly winding down – precisely when the demand for housing was soaring. At the height of the influx of African workers to the cities in 1944, the state did not build any houses for Africans, causing a severe national housing crisis that was most concentrated on the Reef, the area, stretching west and east from Johannesburg, where gold-bearing rock was discovered at the end of the nineteenth century. The number of African families living without accommodation outside locations more than doubled between 1936 and 1951, from 86 000 to 176 000. The historian Doug Hindson has recorded that the Department of Native Affairs in 1947 estimated that an additional 154 185 family houses and 106 877 units for single male workers were required in the urban areas.

These national trends were also reflected in Orlando, which, despite being about thirteen kilometres from the city centre, was emerging as a sought-after location for Johannesburg's growing African urban population. In 1936 the population of the township was estimated at just over 12 000. The official housing waiting list in 1939 stood at a modest 143, suggesting that overcrowding was not a problem, but these figures probably underestimate the actual population, especially the growing number of tenants and sub-tenants, who rented rooms in the houses and backyards of Orlando. One figure cited by Beavon, suggests that the population of Orlando in 1939 was about 35 000. But whatever the precise size of the population in Orlando on the eve of the war, the scale of the housing crisis exploded over the next few years. By 1941 the official housing waiting list had increased to 4 500 and by the end of the war it was 16 000. The number of sub-tenants alone, in the early 1940s, stood at 8 000. Wilfred Thabethe, a Soweto resident, has recalled how this affected households:

> You see, what was happening during those times is that under one roof we used to have extended families – one family. You'd find that you were staying with your uncle from your mother's side and your uncle from your father's side, and your cousins all in one [house], under one roof, you see ... you'd actually find three families under one roof.

Overcrowding and the growing demand for housing laid the basis for the eruption of a squatter movement that forced the dire housing situation facing urban Africans onto the national agenda and prompted the Johannesburg Council and national government to act decisively. The most prominent figure in the squatter movement of Orlando was the charismatic James Mpanza, leader of the Sofasonke Movement.

■ ■ ■ ■ ■

CHAPTER TWO

A RIGHT TO LIVE IN THE CITY

ALTHOUGH HE BECAME A PROMINENT FIGURE IN THE EARLY HISTORY OF Soweto, very little is known about James Mpanza's life prior to his emergence as the leader of a big squatter movement. Mpanza was born in Natal on 15 May 1889. In Pietermaritzburg he attended an Indian school and learnt to speak English and an Indian dialect but, like many of his generation, he was forced to leave school to find work. Through his education he found a job as a clerk at the Durban harbour, and later he worked in Pinetown. It was here that he killed an Indian shopkeeper and was imprisoned in Pietermaritzburg to be executed. But his sentence was first commuted to life and then he was released early. During his imprisonment, the future messianic leader of squatters converted to Christianity. After his release from prison, Mpanza moved to Johannesburg and, like many other new arrivals, he lived in one of the city's slums. In 1934 he moved to Orlando, where he lived at Number 957 Pheele Street. Soon after his arrival in the township, Mpanza was elected onto the advisory board and he emerged as the voice of the growing class of sub-tenants, desperate for their own homes, who had been lobbying the central government and the Johannesburg authorities for years – to no avail – to deal with the shortage of housing.

Frustrated by the lack of response from the authorities, Mpanza mooted the idea of mobilising sub-tenants to occupy open spaces in the location to highlight their plight. His proposal received the cold shoulder from members of the Communist Party, who viewed him with suspicion, but the young

OPPOSITE RIGHT: James 'Sofasonke' Mpanza, the 'father' of Soweto

Source: Wits Historical Papers

members of the African National Congress, who were to become leading figures in the ANC Youth League, were more receptive. Walter Sisulu, one of the founders and leading members of the Youth League, lived with his family in Orlando East. In the book *A Place in the City: The Rand on the Eve of Apartheid*, Walter Sisulu says, 'Mpanza spoke to me and Nelson [Mandela], and said let's pass a resolution at the Orlando Residents' Association. It must be moved by Nelson and seconded by me; in which, he says, that on the 29th January we the residents of Orlando shall evict the sub-tenants. That resolution was moved; and that strategy moved the City Council.'

Mpanza's slogan of 'Housing and Shelter for All' quickly rallied hundreds of sub-tenants, and on 20 March 1944 he led a group of sub-tenants to occupy an empty space on the periphery of Orlando East. There they erected 250 shacks. The act of defiance immediately attracted huge support – the number of families joining the squatter movement increased by 300 a day and within weeks there were 4 000 shacks in the area. Wilfred Thabethe, like many older residents, reveres the role played by Mpanza.

> We used to call that place Zama-Mpanza sacks, because he was the man who was a leader at that time. He is the man who actually started the shacks … This man came, Sofasonke Mpanza, he said there were many people who wanted houses. So he asked all the people who actually wanted houses to come out and build their shacks there, so that the authorities must see that too many people wanted houses. Yes.

Residents called the area 'Masakeng', the place of sacks, because the structures put up by the squatters were made of hessian sacks. The council was now desperate to stave off any further squatting and aimed to wrest control of Masakeng from Mpanza and his Sofasonke Movement by setting up a temporary camp close to Mpanza's shantytown. The temporary camp comprised the most basic accommodation structures, nine metres square, made of breeze blocks, with asbestos roofs but without chimneys or window panes. Mpanza refused to move until the authorities guaranteed to provide permanent housing for the people. But a determined council began to tear down shacks and remove squatters to the new settlement. According to the historian Alf Stadler, 'By the end of May 1944, 200 rooms had been built. By October 1945, 4 042 had been built to accommodate 20 000 people, and the last of the squatters' shacks in "Shantytown", as Mpanza's camp came to be called, had been demolished.'

The squatter movement nonetheless left an indelible mark on urban politics in Johannesburg, showing that direct action by poor black people could force the authorities to respond to their demands. The sub-tenants of

Source: Museum Africa

'Masakeng' — Place of Sacks

Orlando demonstrated unequivocally their determination to have rights in the city, and the most urgent of their rights was access to housing.

The houses built by the council still did not meet the housing needs of the growing population of homeless urban Africans. In January 1946, Mpanza led a second movement of squatters to occupy the incomplete houses in Orlando West. Similar squatter movements sprang up simultaneously across the Reef and, inspired by the example of Mpanza, local leaders from Alexandra, Evaton (Benoni) and other parts of Soweto led land occupations. Squatter movements from Pimville (led by Abel Ntoi), Orlando East (led by Oriel Monongoaha) and Alexandra (led by Schreiner Bhaduza) occupied empty space around Orlando. By the end of 1946, the number of squatters in the area numbered nearly 30 000. The council responded by putting up a number of emergency camps, such as Moroka, and setting aside more land for further housing. More than a thousand families were moved in April 1946 to Jabavu, where another major construction programme consisting of breeze-block houses was started.

The first twenty years of Wilfred Thabethe's life reflected the trials and tribulations of thousands of African families who struggled to make a life for themselves in the city of gold. He was born in 1936 in Bertrams, after which his family moved to Alexandra, probably during the city's clearance of inner city slums. Both his parents were domestic workers in a nursing home.

In 1942, the Thabethe family moved to Orlando where they lived as subtenants and joined Mpanza's movement to fight for a house of their own. But conditions in the settlements were harsh. Wilfred has vivid and lasting memories of the impact of the Highveld rain on their makeshift home:

> In fact we did not realise how bad it was because, truly speaking, we had to stay in the shanty shelters which were called Masakeng. And when it was raining we could not sleep, we had to stand up for the whole night, because of the sacks. Do you understand? It was not roofed with corrugated iron, it was with a sack. And when it was raining the water, the rain, used to come inside the house to the extent that we had to wake up and stand up for the whole night, up until the morning. I felt sorry for my father because he had to go to work the following day. If it was raining for three days, for those three days we could not sleep. We could not sleep ... We used to take some lime, we used to go to the mines and collect some lime to paint the parts of the roof sacks to prevent water from coming in ... And then the lime, if you got a drop of it, was dangerous, because it was burning. It could burn a skin. It was hard, then.

At the first opportunity, the Thabethe family moved from Masakeng to the new settlement, which residents called eMaplatini (plots). According

People queue for homes in Orlando

Source: Museum Africa

to Wilfred Thabethe, 'It was the shelters built by the government. All this area next to Orlando station … were shelters Number Two, Number Three and Number Four shelters. They were divided just below Orlando Stadium on the side of the rail, that was now the shelters. It was in 1947.' Despite promises from the authorities, the amenities, such as toilets and taps, were very limited. 'At the shelters where we stayed,' says Wilfred,'there were no toilets for five years despite everything. We had toilets but they were public toilets, and they were far … next to the shanty township. So we used to walk to the toilets.'

The Thabethe family lived in the area from 1947 to 1954. 'It is then,' recalls Wilfred, 'that the other part of Soweto was [built]. That was Dlamini, Molapo, and other areas. In 1954 my family moved to Dlamini. The stand that we had was a formal house. A four roomed house, with a toilet.'

People came to Orlando and Soweto from all over, journeying to settle in what was to become the country's largest African township. The Matthews' family history highlights the kinds of experiences that typified the lives of urban Africans. Mrs Matthews has talked about her early life:

> I was born in 1921, here in Johannesburg, at a place called Prospect Township. But originally my parents were from Delmas, *ja*. Then we came to Prospect Township, right next to Heidelberg Road. This area was occupied by multinational groups, coloureds, whites, *boers*, everybody. They were moved from Prospect to Orlando East. And life was good there, but we struggled with shopping. The shops were very far. We had to travel a long distance. Jeppe was our nearest town for shopping. So, I was still very young when my parents moved to Orlando. My father was Paul Nkoane and used to travel by horses, selling vegetables to the *boers*. And my mother was Anna Nkoane, the first born of the Thlolwes. She was a domestic worker. We walked to school in Albert Street School at the Wesleyan Church. From there I went to George Goch for my higher primary. Most of the schools were held in church buildings back then. I was introduced to Mr [Philip] Matthews by Khala Andries, his friend. They were both from Kimberley. So, we dated until we got married. We stayed in Sophiatown. From Sophiatown we went to Mzimhlophe, then to Orlando West.

Many families followed a similar route. They would first find a foothold in one of the city's slums, where it was easier to avoid detection by the state. Then they would find their way to one or other of the municipal locations, such as Orlando. Older residents from Orlando West often remember the creation of Masakeng as the time when they moved to the area. Nokuthula

Ramoitheki was born in Orlando West in 1949, at 8357 Twala Street. Her mother came from Bizana in the old Transkei and her father from Natal.

> When my grandparents came here they stayed at the plots … it is where my mother used to stay with her parents. She was pregnant with me when she was staying at the plots. When the *boers* removed them there, Mr Sofasonke brought them here. This is my grandmother's house. I was born here. My mother came here and stayed here. During the process of the removals my father was killed there. I did not know that then. I don't know him. He was killed there.

It appears that, as followers of Mpanza, the Ramoitheki family were part of the movement that occupied the newly built houses in Orlando West in 1946. As the authorities had not yet sold these houses, the new occupants claimed ownership over them. Houses in Orlando West were bigger than those in Orlando East and must have appeared quite luxurious to those living on the government plots. The Mazibuko brothers, whose family hailed from Reitz in the '*Vrystaat*', recall the crammed conditions in Orlando East:

> Yes, it was one room at first and as you looked at it you thought how do I sleep in a one room, but we slept like that. As we grew up then we decided to divide the one room to have kitchen space … In other words you had to build for yourself. If you did not build for yourself it was when you did not have money, and all you did was to divide by a sheet to make a partition. You will then have a room for you and your wife, and the kids sleep in the kitchen.

Not surprisingly, Orlando West quickly became a magnet. Sydney Ramokgopa explains how his family ended up in Orlando West, where he was born in 1950:

> My parents they are from what we call today Limpopo province, from a place called Zoekmekaar … my parents came to Johannesburg I think around 1929. They stayed in Alexandra with one of our relatives and then from Alexandra they got a house in Orlando East … and then, while they were in Orlando East, it was the time when they were building Orlando West, yes. So they came in after Orlando East was completed. Because I was made to understand that the superintendent at the time, he told this old man, that area in Orlando West, the houses are bigger than the ones in Orlando East. In Orlando East it was only two rooms, you see. So then they moved from Orlando East to here. That is why most of the people particularly in this area,

> this side to Mandela side and Sisulu, most of them they are from Orlando East. Yes, they are from Orlando East because they were told that these houses are bigger than those ones in Orlando East, so they came this side.

From the 1940s, Orlando West became one of the sought-after locations. In the early 1940s Walter Sisulu qualified for a house in Phomolong (Number 7372), the new residential area that would develop into Orlando West. As Elinor Sisulu, writing about her parents-in-law, was to say, the new four-roomed house was bigger than the Sisulus' house in Orlando East. 'It had two bedrooms, a kitchen and a small room, which, though it had no bathtub, they called a bathroom because it had a shower enclosure ... the Phomolong house had a tap in the backyard ... cement floors and a ceiling.' Walter Sisulu's comrade, Nelson Mandela, also qualified for a house after the birth of his and his first wife's son in 1946. By the early 1950s Orlando West had assumed the features of a more settled community, as more and more families created homes there.

The electoral victory of the National Party in 1948, however, ushered in a period of mounting uncertainty for urban Africans.

The urban experiences of black people and of Africans in particular were characterised under successive white governments by exclusion,

Source: Museum Africa

Houses in Orlando West were in demand

marginalisation and removals. The state promoted the migrant labour system and therefore sought to limit and control the presence of Africans in urban areas. In other words, the presence of African labour was deemed necessary only insofar as it was required to tend to the needs of white people, and a pivotal part of the state's strategy throughout the twentieth century was to limit African urbanisation through influx control. Those Africans who lived in urban areas were subjected to strict controls, were placed in regimented spaces such as compounds and municipal locations. The policy, which controlled migration from the rural areas and maintained order in the locations, enjoyed limited success until the late 1930s, but after that, as African urbanisation surged ahead, locations were transformed from places intended to exemplify state domination into areas of contestation where urban black working class culture and politics were being forged – and they were to become locales of protest and challenge to white control. As Bonner's and Nieftagodien's research on Alexandra and Ekurhuleni (on the East Rand) shows, popular protest for housing, against pass controls, high rents and bus fare hikes affected locations across the Reef in the 1940s.

In response to the upsurge of location-based popular struggles and a wave of industrial actions in the 1940s, the state attempted to re-assert control over the urban black population. It was in fact a salient feature, from 1948 onwards, of the apartheid government, which pursued the policies of urban reconfiguration – forced removals, creation of group areas and townships – with much greater determination than had its predecessors. A key aim behind the creation of new townships was to establish basic conditions for the stabilisation of urban African labour, such as the provision of accommodation and elementary education. In this way, the growing demand by industry for reliable and cheap unskilled and semi-skilled labour could more easily be met. State policies in the 1950s were premised on the recognition that some Africans could be permanently urbanised, so the National Party ideologues emphasised – and aimed to entrench – a distinction between African urban 'insiders' and 'outsiders'. 'Insiders', from the perspective of the apartheid government, were those Africans who qualified under the so-called 'Section 10' laws to work and live legitimately in urban areas where they were given access to public housing in segregated townships. According to 'Section 10' of the Natives Laws Amendment Act of 1952, Africans qualified for the right to residence in urban areas if they met certain conditions, such as working continuously for the same employer for a decade or being born and living continuously in an urban area for at least fifteen years. Their right to a degree of permanence in the urban areas was based on the state's belief, at the time, that some Africans could be 'detribalised' and thus permanently urbanised. By contrast, 'outsiders' were deemed to be 'tribal' (implying 'rural') and were consigned to a life of migrancy. Their presence in the urban areas depended on work contracts of specified durations, which means they were required to return to the 'homelands', the rural areas, when their contracts expired. The state's acceptance of the permanent presence of some Africans in the urban areas was a *qualified* concession. It was also a policy shift, in response to the growing demands for labour from the booming secondary economy and also, critically, to the struggles waged by urban Africans in the 1940s, in which the squatter movements played a pivotal role. On the one hand, industry required a reliable and relatively cheap workforce. On the other hand, the state was determined to break urban political militancy. Both wanted the urban African working class brought under control.

One of the strategies the government used to achieve this objective was the establishment of new townships. HF Verwoerd, who was at the time the minister of native affairs, and has become known as the 'architect of apartheid', explained the government's views in a press release announcing the formation of the Mentz Committee in 1952.

> Squatter chaos, overcrowding of existing Native plots, illegal lodging in white yards, the removal of those who refuse to work and thus don't belong in the city, can only be combated once large enough legal townships for Natives are established close to the towns ... The most complicated problem of this character in the Union, exists in the area from the north in Pretoria to the Vaal River, and in the east from Springs till far in the west to Krugersdorp and Randfontein ...

From the 1950s, the state embarked on a massive programme of reconfiguring the urban areas along racial lines. It appointed the Mentz Commission (also known as the 'black spots' commission) to formulate a plan. The commission recommended that all so-called black spots be removed and replaced with what it called regional group areas and townships. What this meant was that old locations such as Sophiatown, Dukathole and Cato Manor, where urban black people had built communities for several decades, would be destroyed and their residents relocated to racially defined areas such as Soweto, Lenasia and Eldorado Park. Perhaps the best-known example was the forced removal of thousands of people from Sophiatown to Meadowlands in 1954/55. From the state's perspective, the creation of what it called 'regional model townships' was the most effective way of monitoring and therefore controlling large African populations, and careful planning went into the creation of new townships.

In 1952, in a speech to the Senate, Verwoerd set out the government's vision for the future siting and planning of African townships. The site should be at an adequate distance from the European town and should preferably adjoin the location of a neighbouring town, so as to decrease rather than increase the number of Native areas. The site should preferably be separated from the European area by an industrial buffer, where industries existed or were being planned. The site should have provision for an adequate hinterland for expansion, stretching away from the European area, and it should be within easy distance of the town or city for transport purposes – by rail rather than by road. There should be a road, preferably running through the industrial areas, connecting the location site with the city. The location site should possess open buffer zones around it, the breadth of which would depend on whether the location bordered upon a densely or sparsely occupied European area. Finally, it should be at a considerable distance from main, and more particularly national, roads, 'the use of which as local transport routes for the location should be totally discouraged'.

Between the early 1950s and mid-1960s the state built thousands of houses in African townships, as well as in coloured and Indian group areas. For people who lived as tenants and sub-tenants in the old locations this was often welcome, as they were able to gain access to their own homes for the first time. But the houses were small, consisting of one or two bedrooms, and they were located on small plots. New townships were deliberately established far from the white cities, forcing residents to incur high costs and huge inconveniences to get to their workplaces. The destruction of old communities caused deep resentment, especially among property owners who were aggrieved by the loss of homes in which they had invested time and money, and which were generally more spacious than the matchbox houses in the new townships.

In the old locations, these properties were also vital sources of income from rentals and this was yet another cause, as in the Sophiatown campaign, of the widespread opposition to forced removals. The state, however, was determined to implement its plans, and to use force. By the late 1950s, tens of thousands of people were relocated to the new townships. Soweto mushroomed during this time as a result of mass housing provision funded by the state and through a loan of six million rands from the Anglo American Corporation. In the decade from 1955 to 1965 approximately 4 400 houses a year were built in Soweto. New areas such as Dlamini, Chiawelo, Emdeni, Phiri and Zola were created. By 1966 Soweto had emerged as the largest African township in the country, with an estimated 87 500 houses.

■ ■ ■ ■ ■

Source: Museum Africa

Soweto expanded rapidly from the 1950s

CHAPTER THREE

PLACE OF DEFIANCE

Source: Bailey's African History Archive

Defiance Campaign

ALTHOUGH THE MASS PROVISION OF HOUSING WAS LINKED TO ITS acceptance of the presence of Africans in the cities, the government was also explicit in that it was not conceding any substantial rights to Africans. The state's attempts to assert control over every aspect of the lives of black people, to deny them political rights, and to enforce its policies through coercion and violence, inevitably generated resistance. These processes – increasing oppression on one side counterbalanced by resistance on the other – became more pronounced after the advent of apartheid in 1948. As soon as it came to power, the National Party began formulating laws to impose complete racial segregation and control over the black population.

In 1950, several pieces of legislation such as the Group Areas Act and the Suppression of Communism Act were promulgated to give effect to the state's agenda. It quickly became apparent to the black population that the apartheid government was prepared to act ruthlessly, not only to realise the ideological goal of racial segregation but also to suppress oppositional voices.

A new spirit of defiance had, however, taken root among the urban population since the early 1940s, and it had radicalised. In May 1950, the Communist Party of South Africa, the CPSA, and from July that same year, the African National Congress mobilised mass protests against these laws, inaugurating a decade of resistance against apartheid. The ANC was by this time under the leadership of younger and more radical activists, and had adopted a programme of action in 1949 which laid the political basis for its involvement in mass mobilisation and defiance. In the process it emerged as the most prominent national political organisation in the country. The Defiance Campaign of 1952 marked the high point of this mass resistance.

Orlando featured prominently in the mass struggles of the 1950s, as a site of struggle and because several of the key figures in the emerging national mass movement lived in the area. For example, Walter Sisulu became secretary general of the ANC in 1950, Nelson Mandela became the volunteer-in-chief of the defiance campaign, and Albertina Sisulu emerged as a prominent figure in the women's movement – in the ANC Women's League and, from 1954, also in the Federation of South African Women. The Orlando branches of the ANC and the Women's and Youth Leagues played increasingly influential roles.

Mrs Matthews remembers that there were not too many women activists in the area, 'but there were some who were very active, like Martha Mothopeng. You would find her in each and every meeting.' Laughing, she adds, 'They used to call her madam speaker.' Throughout the 1950s, mobilisation in the principal campaigns was mounted by activists and enjoyed considerable support from residents. For example, in response to the introduction of Bantu Education in 1954, several communities established cultural clubs (or unregistered schools) offering an alternative education to children. Elinor Sisulu recalls that one of these was created in the Sisulu house in Orlando and that her mother-in-law Albertina Sisulu played a key role, together with other activists, in mobilising widespread support from the broader community.

A year later, many of these activists campaigned for the collection of demands for the Congress of the People that was held in nearby Kliptown in June 1955. After the very successful mass gathering at which the Freedom Charter was adopted, the state moved decisively to undermine the Congress Alliance which consisted of the ANC and its allies, the South African Congress of Trade Unions, the Natal and Transvaal Indian Congresses, the Coloured People's Congress and the Congress of Democrats. The Freedom Charter was adopted by delegates from all over the country who met at Kliptown, only a few kilometres from Orlando, and contained many of the main demands of the liberation movement: for democracy, jobs, housing and education for all. Many of the key Congress Alliance leaders were rounded up and charged with treason. The ensuing trial went on for nearly four years, from 1956 to 1960, and effectively deprived the movement of its most senior and capable leaders. Mandela and other leading figures from Orlando were among the 156 accused. Philip Matthews, a local activist who rose to prominence in the Orlando ANC branch, was also incarcerated. Again, Mrs Matthews' words show how the manner of his arrest and the trial left a lasting impression on his family.

> By the time the police came to arrest them, my child, yo! It was bitter, terrible … the cries and screaming of women and children. Believe me, it was very sad. I remember Barbara, my daughter, I think she was this age then [demonstrating her height by hand]. After my husband had been arrested she cried bitterly. 'Mama, why do we leave papa here? Why doesn't he come home with us?' By the way, she was seeing her father for the first time, ever since he got arrested. She saw him in court at the synagogue. So she did not understand why he was not coming home with us. Motswaledi, Sisulu, and many others were there.

The Orlando branch of the Women's League also played a significant role in the mobilisation against the extension of passes to African women. On 9 August 1956, Albertina and her fellow League comrades came to Pretoria, in a train full of women from Orlando and other parts of Soweto, to join their comrades from all over the country in the historic march to the Union Buildings. The state, however, ignored the women's pleas and soon began stepping up the issuing of passes to African women. Women's organisations responded by resisting and defying the state. In 1958, nurses at Baragwanath hospital stridently objected to carrying passes as it would have a disastrous effect on the whole administration of hospitals and clinics. In Orlando, Albertina Sisulu and Winnie Mandela were instrumental in the ANC Women's League demonstration. Mrs Matthews recalls what happened during the local anti-pass campaign.

> The whole area was full of passes, women, children and everybody. Oh, yes! They would go around collecting them, yes. Well, it was up to you if you wanted to give it to them. Some people would hide theirs and some would hand theirs over. They would bring a certain amount of paraffin and set all the passes on fire. That's where they burned the passes.

These actions resulted in the arrest of hundreds of women, about 1 200 of whom were imprisoned at the Fort in Johannesburg where they were, in the words of Elinor Sisulu, 'crammed like sardines in filthy cells.' But despite the heroic stand by these African women, the state eventually imposed its hated pass system on them.

Although national campaigns increasingly became the focus of local political organisations and preoccupied many of the key activists, local 'bread and butter' issues occasionally became rallying points for political mobilisation. The rent boycott in Orlando, in the mid-1950s, was one of them. In 1954, the government announced new rentals for African families. Families

Source: Wits Historical Papers

Women protest against passes, 1956

earning more than fifteen pounds a month would have to pay the economic rentals of two pounds ten shillings. The level of sub-economic rentals was also increased. Residents of Orlando responded by mounting a boycott of the economic rentals. The campaign was spearheaded by the Orlando Rent Protest Committee, whose leader was George Xorile with the active support of the ANC and the CPSA members. Xorile's committee successfully contested the proposed introduction of economic rentals in court, winning acclaim in the community. This struggle continued for four more years until 1958, when the courts finally rejected an appeal by the committee, after which the boycott fell apart, leaving boycotters with rent arrears bills.

Mrs Masoma, an elderly resident from Orlando, remembers her mother as an enthusiastic supporter of the rent boycott but that she nearly lost her house because the family was unable to pay the arrears that had accumulated as a result of the boycott. The family put up a desperate fight when the authorities moved to repossesses their home. According to Mrs Masoma, the superintendent conceded on condition that they were to pay the economic rent arrears.

Xorile and his comrades also founded the Asinamali Party, which successfully contested the advisory board elections against James Mpanza's Sofasonke Party (Mpanza had opposed the boycott action, losing considerable support in the community). This struggle reflected an important shift in the politics of Orlando. Until the late 1940s, Mpanza was

Photograph by Peter Magubane. Courtesy Wits Historical Papers

Robert Sobukwe, leader of PAC arrested in Orlando

Source:

undoubtedly the most important political figure in the area and enjoyed enormous support as the leader of the squatter movement. Then he was eclipsed by a younger and more militant group of activists who were prepared to defy the state and to link local struggles to the broader political resistance against apartheid.

Thoughout the 1950s, and especially after the adoption of the Freedom Charter in 1955, the Africanist wing of the ANC campaigned vigorously against what they perceived to be the leaders' 'multiracial' politics. Orlando became a principal site of contestation between young Africanists and the established ANC leadership. Most of the leaders of the Africanist opposition in the ANC were drawn from members of the Youth League in Orlando and included Zeph Mothopeng, Potlake Leballo and Peter Raboroko. According to the political scientist Tom Lodge in a seminal work on black politics, the three had lost their jobs during the defiance campaign and the struggles against Bantu Education. Mothopeng was born in 1916, had a BA degree and was the president of the Transvaal African Teachers' Association. Raboroko, a founding member of the ANC Youth League, was regarded as one of the main theorists of the Africanist movement, and wrote regularly on matters related to the revival of African culture.

The Orlando Youth League branch was one of the biggest in the country, and was influential in the politics of the broader movement. Africanists occupied leading positions in the branch and used it as a platform to express their ideas. As a result, the ANC in Orlando became the site of intense contestation between the emerging group of Africanists and the established leadership. Tensions between the different factions in the ANC reached a climax at the Transvaal provincial conference in 1958, which resulted in the Africanists' decision to formally secede from the ANC and to create a new movement. The new party, the Pan Africanist Congress, the PAC, was officially launched in Orlando.

Soon after its launch, the PAC, now under the leadership of Robert Sobukwe, launched its own anti-pass campaign, which culminated in major demonstrations on 21 March 1960. On that fateful day, the police opened fire on protesters in Sharpeville, killing sixty-nine people and injuring many more. The Sharpeville massacre marked a decisive turning point in the country's history. A couple of weeks later, on April 8, the state banned the ANC and the PAC. In August of the same year it declared the first national state of emergency and embarked on the systematic repression of the anti-apartheid movement. Activists were forced underground and into exile in order to keep the liberation movements afloat. Importantly, within eighteen months of the massacre the ANC and PAC both launched their armed struggles against the state with the founding of their respective military wings, Umkhonto we Sizwe (MK) and Poqo.

Mandela was appointed commander-in-chief of MK and Sisulu played a pivotal role in the high command of MK and in keeping together the remnants of the ANC in the underground. Both Mandela and Sisulu were key targets of the state, and after two years of successfully evading the police they were eventually arrested.

They became the most prominent members in the Rivonia trial, in which the leadership of the ANC and Umkhonto we Sizwe were found guilty and sentenced to life imprisonment, and it was due to their leading role that the state went out of its way to harass the Sisulu and Mandela families in Orlando. The Mandela house, like those of other activists, had endured regular raids by the security police – and the raids increased significantly after Sharpeville. When Mandela became the pivotal underground leader of the ANC, his house was placed under almost twenty-four hour surveillance and raids were carried out at all times of the day and night.

Winnie Mandela's every move was closely monitored. 'Our house,' Winnie has said, 'was an extension of the police station, every day they came; the children were petrified. No amount of explanation could reassure them because I had no protection.' Within a couple of years Number 8115 in Orlando had been transformed from a centre of resistance into an effective prison, and Winnie bore the brunt of the state's attention.

The Sisulu house was similarly affected. Albertina Sisulu was the first female to be arrested under the ninety days detention law (the General Laws Amendment Act of 1963), followed by her neighbour and fellow comrade in the Federation of South African Women, Rose Mbele. The state's determination to destroy the families of political activists became even more evident when the Sisulus' 17-year-old son, Max, was also detained under the same law. With both parents unable to earn a living, the Sisulu members of the household were under severe pressure, as Elinor Sisulu has subsequently written, simply to sustain themselves. It was support from neighbours, whose gestures of goodwill put them in danger of harassment by the security forces, that allowed the families of activists to survive through those dark days.

The police harassed all the known activists to intimidate them and to break their spirits. They routinely raided the Matthews house to take Philip Matthews in for questioning. Mrs Matthews recalls:

> Oh, but they [police] used to like him [Mr Matthews] very much. When they came they would take him with them. I cannot recall how many times they took him with them, four times or so. They would take him. Bring him back. Take him again, you know. He was in and out of jail, all that.

And in her opinion not everyone supported the political activists.

> There were many of them, the sell-outs, who hated Matthews very much. They would even go and report him to the Special Branch and to the police so that he could get arrested. There were plenty of spies, my child: whites, blacks, Tswanas, coloureds. *Hulle was baie.* Somebody would come and pretend to be a member of the party or a member of their group, only to find that they were just spying to get information out of us. So we became aware of that.

Philip Matthews was sentenced to twelve years in prison and was released in 1972. As the jackboot of state repression came crashing down on the liberation movements, many male activists were forced to operate underground or to go into exile. Under the circumstances, women activists such as Albertina Sisulu, Winnie Mandela, Lilian Ngoyi and Helen Joseph kept the liberation flames burning, even as many of them had to endure constant police harassment and had to struggle to maintain their families. Mrs Matthews remembers women holding meetings in Orlando to discuss:

> … about our arrested leaders. That we must stand up and do something in order to get them released. To organise a march to John Vorster Square and demand their immediate release. I am telling you, Winnie was brave. She was one of the ring-leaders. She really looked down upon them [police]. She would shout at them, 'What the hell are you looking at?' [laughs]. Same applies when we were having our meetings by the mountain. These *boers* would just barge in uninvited. And Winnie would say to us, 'What do these things want here? Are they also in the meeting?' Yo! We would all laugh. And they would just look at her. Then we decided not to have a meeting any more.

These individual acts of bravery and defiance notwithstanding, by the mid-1960s the state had succeeded in substantially weakening the liberation movements, largely through repression but also by a slew of new laws aimed at undermining the position of Africans in urban areas.

■ ■ ■ ■ ■

CHAPTER FOUR

UNCERTAIN TIMES

FROM THE LATE 1950S, THE GOVERNMENT SHIFTED ITS IDEOLOGICAL orientation to pursue a doctrinaire form of apartheid. The period from 1960 to the early 1970s is regarded as the era of 'high apartheid' characterised by the National Party's attempts to halt and reverse African immigration to urban areas, its promotion of the homelands system, and the entrenchment of the migrant labour system by, among other interventions, a stricter enforcement of pass laws and the construction of migrant hostels in urban townships. Key features of urban township life now came under attack by the state. Home ownership was the primary target. The removal of the old locations effectively eliminated freehold title for the vast majority of Africans. In the new townships, the state introduced the thirty-year leasehold scheme, which gave households a degree of 'ownership' for a given period, and a measure of security in the urban areas. But, as HF Verwoerd intimated in 1956, the state was determined not to convey to Africans any sense that they could expect to enjoy basic rights in the urban areas. Anticipating the important policy changes that would come into effect from the late 1950s, the 'architect of apartheid' explained in his speech to the fifth annual conference of the Institute of Administrators of Non-European Affairs, in September 1956, that,

> The Native cannot acquire any property rights in the European area and therefore also not in the Location or Native Township. He cannot acquire any freehold rights there because that would clash

with the basic principle of separation and separate development. On the other hand he can certainly acquire certain forms of possession which do not have any characteristics of permanency, such as home ownership and even home ownership based on a lease of the land on which the house is erected for a guaranteed number of years. He can acquire this because there is nothing in it which imports to it anything of the essence of permanency such as property ownership.

In the 1960s, even the limited concessions made to Africans in the early 1950s, such as home ownership in the new townships, came under attack and in 1968 the government summarily terminated leasehold rights in Soweto where approximately 10 000 homes were held under the thirty-year lease scheme. The position of African women was especially precarious. For example, in 1967, as the historians Philip Bonner and Lauren Segal record in their history of Soweto, 'the government ordered that widows, unmarried mothers, divorced women and deserted wives could not keep their names on the waiting list for a house. Furthermore, a widowed or divorced woman could not be allowed to remain in a house registered under her husband's name.'

The implications of this shift in policy were far-reaching for African women. Not only did they face greater dangers than males of being deported to a homeland – their access to the most basic right, a home, was made dependent on their relationship with men. Clement Twala provided Bonner and Segal with a vivid explanation of the dilemmas faced by African women in Soweto:

> Women were not allowed to become heads of families. If your husband dies, you'd have to get your son to be head of the family and, if he was too young, you had to get a close male relative to occupy the house. If a woman failed to get a man to take up tenancy, the house would be declared vacant and the woman had to go back to her place of origin or live as a lodger in other people's homes.

Pass laws and permits gave the state enormous control over African people. Municipal police or 'blackjacks', employers, housing officials and other state bureaucrats collectively monitored various aspects of township life. Yet people found ways of getting around the system, often with the assistance of local officials. Shadrack Mutau, who grew up in Orlando West, explains how he managed to navigate the system:

> … when I was supposed to write my JC [Junior Certificate] only to find that I did not have a permit because my father had left us. According to apartheid law both my parents were supposed to be pre-

sent. So I was staying with my sister ... I did not have a place I called home. Due to the help of the gods, plans were made. I met Bra Joe in Orlando. He was the one who was in charge of organising permits for people. He made plans by organising a permit for me, even though it was not an official one. I remember quite well in 1966 while I was working at Computer Suppliers Corporation most of the people did not have passbooks. Because it was seventy-two hours they got arrested. I remember I went to the pass office and I was given my qualification, which entitled me to work. I was given the GP5. I worked with that GP5 for a while. I realised that being without proper home is not good. I went back to Bra Joe and we lied about some of the things and we got it fine. It took me a while and I got a 10 (1B). That 10 (1B) entitled me to have a house. But you were supposed to get married first. So I got married to Mkhize's daughter at Emdeni.

At the same time as the government built houses in the townships to accommodate urban African families, it also embarked on the construction of single-sex migrant hostels close to industrial areas and in the new townships; this was in large part to eliminate the presence of African workers living in white areas, in what were called 'locations in the sky' (literally, domestic rooms on the roofs of residential buildings, but also domestic quarters in white suburbs). In 1953, the Johannesburg Council found that approximately 25 000 African men were living in apartment blocks

Applying for passes at Albert Street pass office

Source: Bailey's African History Archive

and domestic quarters and quickly formulated plans to eliminate such 'irregular' accommodation. In 1956 the state promulgated the infamous Native (Urban Areas) Amendment Act, also known as the 'Locations in the Sky Act', which aimed to remove African cleaners from the city to the newly constructed Dube Hostel. There were thousands of migrants whom the state wanted to accommodate outside the township proper, so as to maintain their migrant status and to avoid the responsibility of housing them and their families. Nancefield and Mzimhlophe hostels were built to cater for them. Until the mid-1960s, the state invested huge sums in the development of urban townships, but thereafter funds were channelled to the so-called 'homelands', especially to prop up the Bantustan bureaucracies, and as a result townships were neglected. Conditions deteriorated.

In the period from the early 1950s to the early 1970s there were rapid and fundamental changes to the lives of Sowetans. Not only did the state impose tight control and surveillance of people's lives, implementing policies that stripped Africans of the remaining vestiges of their basic rights – it also promoted the policies of 'separate development' and 'tribal identities' by subjecting the townships created from the late 1950s to ethnic zoning. Orlando was not carved up into ethnic areas because it was created prior to the formulation of this policy. However, in the 1960s the state insisted on the establishment of ethnically-based schools. This was the socio-political context within which new communities were forged in the townships of the 1960s.

These new communities were made up different groups who were forced into the same residential space: old and new urbanites, people who had been removed from old locations, and immigrants to Johannesburg from different rural localities. When they were moved into their new houses, most people in Soweto simply did not know their neighbours. Life in these townships was initially quite fragmented and lacked the kind of social cohesion that had been produced in the old locations or in rural communities. These were the kind of circumstances that generated social alienation, which was most pronounced among young people.

Youth identities and subcultures were an important part of social life in Soweto from the late 1950s. A common feature of youth identity was the strong emphasis on being urban. In his book *Bo-Tsotsi*, the historian Clive Glaser says that the two most popular subcultures in Soweto in the 1960s and early 1970s were the 'clevers' and the 'ivies'. 'Clevers' were characterised by an assertive 'urbanness' reflected in 'dress, language and style codes'. Gangsters were generally regarded as clevers, although not all clevers were gangsters. The ivies were usually employed and not involved in criminal activities. In an interview, talking from his experience, Alfred Jacobs maintains that '... a person was recognised by the way he dressed and they would say *dis 'n clever* [this is a clever]'. 'Those were the times of the Sureshells,' claims Jacobs. 'The eight piece caps, when you were not a clever, you won't know how to wear a cap, but if you were a clever, you wore a cap ... There were very few people that cut their hair to *chiskop* [bald head]. We the people that had hair wore a Dobbs.'

Another sharp distinction that emerged among the youth during this period was between the Ndofaya and Kalkoene. In an interview, Colin Nxumalo explains:

> By the time the group from Meadowlands came, they came in 1955, when they got here they were from Sophiatown and Newclare. They called us *singamakalkuni* (Afrikaans '*kalkoene*', English 'turkey') they said because, they don't hear us when we talk, they said '*die kalkoene, die is kal, kal, kal*'. But then we used to fight with those boys, we even took out knives and fought with stones, then you'll never hear anything about *amakalkune*. We called them the Ndofaya because they were from Sophiatown.

The Ndofayas originated from the Western Areas and grew up speaking 'tsotsitaal' that was influenced by Afrikaans, whereas the slang spoken by the youth who grew up in Soweto, the *kalkoene*, was influenced more strongly by Zulu, according to Glaser. These divisions, and the shaping of youth identities, reflected the broader process of community construction in Soweto. Arguably, one of the most significant expressions of this phenomenon was the proliferation of gangs during the period spanning the late 1950s to the early 1970s.

The economic boom of the 1960s increased the demand for black labour which, coupled with stricter influx control, meant almost full employment for adults, especially those prepared to do unskilled and semi-skilled jobs. But unemployment levels remained unusually high among the township youth. According to Glaser, the factors contributing to this state of affairs included that many youths were not registered and found it difficult to get employment as bosses were generally not prepared to employ anyone without the appropriate documents. Another factor was that employers regarded urban youth as unreliable, and preferred employing workers from the rural areas. And then, township youth despised hard and low-paid work.

The Bantu Education Act introduced primary schooling to large numbers of African children – by the mid-1960s it was estimated that eighty per cent of African children between the ages of seven and fourteen were attending school. However, funding for African education in urban areas was drastically reduced during this period as the government diverted funds to build educational institutions in the homelands, and the construction of

Source: Bailey's African History Archive

Source: Community Collection

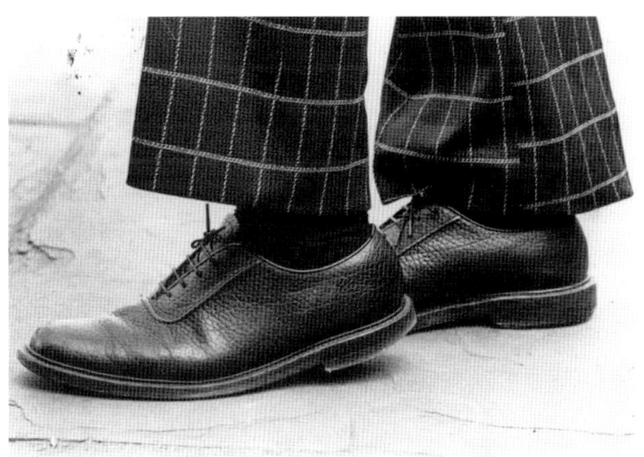

Source: Bailey's African History Archive

LEFT & TOP RIGHT: Youth subcultures flourished in the 1960's

BELOW RIGHT: Fashion ...

new schools in Soweto came almost to a standstill. This was especially so for the building of secondary schools, which had always lagged far behind the building of primary schools. The eight secondary schools in Soweto were terribly overcrowded, and many of those who completed primary school simply could not continue with their schooling. Under the circumstances, young people, especially males, were faced with very uncertain futures. Added to that, the township was bereft of any meaningful social and recreational facilities, which meant that the large numbers of unemployed and out-of-school young men had a lot of free, or idle, time on their hands. These were ideal conditions for the proliferation of gangs.

According to Mbulelo Mbele, 'Gangsterism was a huge thing in Jozi especially in Soweto'.

> Each township had a specific gang or group that was known throughout the township. In White City it was the Damaras, in Killarney it was the Eagles, and in Orlando it was the Vikings and later on the Kwaitos. These youngsters don't know where the word kwaito comes from. The coloured people used to refer to well dressed people as being '*kwaai*'. There used to be huge fights among these groups and they would fight and compete over clothes and girlfriends.

Almost every section of Soweto had a gang. Some areas had several. Wilfred Thabethe remembers that at one point '… the gangsters here in Orlando West … used to call themselves Dambuza Ranch. In Orlando East, we had what we called Plantation Spoilers. In Mzimhlophe we had the Hazels, and in White City, we had the Black Swines.' The Black Swines and the Pirates were among the dominant gangs in the early 1960s, operating largely in the Mofolo and Jabavu areas but it seems to have been Orlando that was a favourite choice of battlefield between the rival gangs, particularly in the late 1950s.

Gangs were distinguishable by their style of clothing, something into which they put considerable effort. Everyone knew what the gangs wore. The Mazibuko brothers said that '… we could see the Pirates by the *doeks* that they put around the heads with horns. The Black Swines had their caps turned backwards and all carrying weapons like knives, *imikhonto* [spears], *imbazo* [axes].' Mbulelo Mbele recalls how much importance the gangs attached to style:

> Then there were the Kwaitos, [it] started here in Orlando. Coloureds were Makwais, you were supposed to dress up nicely … coloured … you see, *kwaai*… the Vikings were the best dressers, they even liked to boast. When they come to Mzimhlophe, if there is a stokvel they

> would hire a car, for only a short distance ... Dodge ... and Chev. Hey, they were smart, they liked to boast. Their cars would drop them off ... then go to fetch another group with their girlfriends, then they will drink and drink. Then the others start to be jealous now, they will chase one of the patrons and that person will run around until his transport leaves him behind, they will be running around in search of buildings, hey, they used to fight in the bush, man.

In the late 1950s there were two prominent gangs in Orlando East, the Apaches and the Berliners. They were bitter rivals and often fought pitched battles. The Apaches disintegrated after the arrest of numerous members in the early 1960s. At around this time the Kwaitos rose to prominence in Orlando, and the Kwaitos and Vikings remained the main gangs in Orlando into the 1970s.

Gangs fought over territory, but more often than not they fought over women. The Mazibuko brothers explain:

> They were fighting about girlfriends ... they would come from other sides to claim the girlfriends. [T]hey were fighting seriously over these girls. You could not come from Dube for example and come for a girl this side. You would be in trouble ... It was better if you came with the gang... If they [found] the girl they were looking for, then they would take the girl and go with her.

Perhaps the most well-known gang of the late 1960s and early 1970s was the Hazels, led by 'Bra Forker' and Clifford Mashiloane, and which originated in the Mzimhlophe area. At the height of their power, the Hazels had a core membership of about thirty and imposed a reign of terror on the railway line between Soweto and Johannesburg. Young people knew which parts of the township, or trains, to avoid. 'We had no transport that time', says Colin Nxumalo, and therefore,

> ... we walked to the station, we knew that this space is for so and so, when we ride the train at Phefeni or ride London. We didn't call it Orlando we called it London. No, no, no I'm going to ride at London, I'm not going to Phefeni today, I'm going to ride at London, the coach was well known. There came a group from Pimville, they also had their place, so we never used to cross against each other. So that's how we grew up.

According to Mbulelo Mbele the power of the Hazels was broken after a bloody fight at a railway station:

> In the early seventies a tragic event happened here at Mzimhlophe Station. The Hazels were involved in a huge fight with a rival gang from Naledi. When the train stopped the Hazels went inside and started killing people. A lot of innocent people died that day. That was the downfall of the Hazels because many were shot and arrested. Many of the core group members went to prison for a very long time.

By the early 1960s crime in Soweto had escalated, although Orlando West was not as badly affected as areas such as Zola, which became known as *slagpale* (abbatoir). It was estimated that the murder rate in Soweto in 1960 was four times higher than in Chicago. But the South African police were far more interested in enforcing apartheid laws than in combating crime in African townships, and some of the older residents established Makgotla, a group of older men who policed the township, responsible for curbing crime by apprehending criminals, bringing them before a court of the Makgotla, and meting out punishment to those found guilty.

But even if crime and gangs instilled fear in the lives of Sowetan residents it would be wrong to imagine that life in the new township was dominated by gangsterism. Mbulelo Mbele acknowledges that most young people encountered gangsters in almost every aspect of their lives – but that did not detract from having fun and organising parties.

> Apart from that [gangs], life at that time was very good. People used to love having fun. There were special parties called 'sessions'. These sessions were only for top people in society. Not anyone could attend these sessions. A group of gangsters used to come with their girlfriends and they would buy a lot of booze and food. They would count the amount of money they spent in your session and it was compulsory for you to spend just as much, or even more, at their sessions as well.
>
> The sad part was that not very many of these parties would end without someone getting shot or stabbed at that time. It was as if life was worthless at the time. But stabbing was the more prevalent way of killing. People would fight and kill each other over the most nonsensical of issues. However, people used to generate a lot of income from these sessions. When your session was done you could buy a car – that's how much money they used to make from these parties.

■ ■ ■ ■ ■

CHAPTER FIVE

GOOD TIMES

IN ORLANDO, AS ELSEWHERE IN SOWETO, SOCIAL LIFE TENDED TO CENTRE on shebeens and local clubs. This was true even in Mpanza's shantytown, as the Mazibuko brothers recalled.

> It was the shelters, then the Masakeng, and as you go forward from that place there were spots where people used to have their drinks even though we did not drink then. The liquor that was drunk at that time, they used to dig it in holes.Yes, and they did that so that the police could not arrest the sellers. 'There comes the police,' we would say. That beer was dug underground and remained cold always. They will close the holes again and seal it so that the police cannot even trace the beer underground. A person who went to that house to buy beer was expected to open the ground and pour beer for himself. You went there to buy carrying your money, the old lady will take the money and a person would go and dig for his beer because the old lady did not want to involve herself with being arrested. A person went to pour beer for himself even if he can pour more for himself … the risk was his. If the police find you in the hole, they arrest you … but it was nice, man.

In the established areas such as Orlando West a more sophisticated culture of indulgence took root, as Wilfred Thabethe noted.

> We used to go to the Pelican. And there were some chosen shebeens … yes, Club Pelican. And we had some shebeens around Orlando East. We had to go to Rockville, there was Rowena's place and Lekodi.

The Pelican Club in the 1970s became one of the main centres of musical entertainment in Orlando and the broader Soweto. Rita Tandy reminisces in an interview, and recalls the day her brother, who had been overseas for a long time, returned home and decided to open the club:

> He came back and said, 'You know, I want to live a quiet life.' And then he decided to open a night club. The name Pelican – it's amazing how people refer to it as a bird, it was never actually a bird. He was just sitting around with friends and said, we are going to open this night club, and so on, and we have a building, you know, my parents' place. They said 'Never! No! The government will never allow you to do this. Open this? After all we are not even allowed to drink liquor.' So, he said 'Phel-I-can!' and that's how the name Pelican came about.

It took the authorities several months to give permission for the club to be opened. Pelican attracted people from all over Johannesburg – and beyond. According to Rita even white people frequented the place, which unfortunately gave the authorities an excuse to raid it regularly. In fact, soon after the opening, on a Friday night, '… they were here and they surrounded the place with pick-up trucks,' says Rita.

> We had the first black ambassador in the country, he was from Malawi and he was here. They arrested everybody. They took him to the police station. The fact that he was a diplomat, they didn't care. They said 'Black people must know their place. *Kaffers* must know their place.' We were arrested.

Despite harassment from the police the Pelican flourished. 'Sunday was cabaret night. People came from everywhere. It was really fantastic. The place would be so full, packed.' It also quickly became one of the main venues where local artists performed. According to Rita:

> All these musicians started here. Sipho Hotstix started here, they stayed here in the basement, Khaya Mahlangu, Mankunku, really good musicians, like Bheki Mseleku.

Source: Sally Gaule

'The Pelican Club'

Orlando was a centre of social and cultural activity, with Uncle Tom's Hall hosting a wide variety of music groups and plays. The renowned Gibson Kente staged numerous plays in the hall, transforming the space into a mecca of township and protest theatre. From the late 1960s especially, there was a proliferation of musical and theatre performances in various venues. Colin Nxumalo:

> Uncle Tom's Hall, Mavis Isaacson, Orlando Communal Hall, eh, BMSC [Bantu Men's Social Club] in town, and where we used to get our passes from at Polly street. They used to perform in all these halls … on Sunday afternoons.

But in Colin's mind there is no doubt which was the main venue. 'Yes, Uncle Tom's Hall, it was still *the* hall. This was also where the local group, the Markhams, performed. Founding members of the group, the Mazibuko brothers, explain its development:

Source: Community Collection

Orlando West was seen as a middle class suburb

> We started as two people because we loved music but it was not very easy. We recruited other people whom we thought loved music as well, until we were four people. Then we were a combo and singing and practising every day. Yes, there were other groups but we were known as local people and the security guards at the hall knew us. That was the name of the music, the Markhams brothers … It was our manager Mr Hendrick who liked this name … It was just a sexy uniform where we put on white trousers, takkies and a jacket. We would take music from the radio and compose it to suit the audience. Monday to Friday we were practising and if there was something that was going to happen over the weekend, we would sing there. Uncle Tom's Hall. We were going out to places like the bioscope and sometimes you would dress up to check your girlfriends. That time you had more than one girlfriend, one maybe in Dube, one in Mndeni and that time we were nicely dressed. We would go as far as Mzimhlophe, checking girlfriends.

Throughout the 1960s and 1970s the Orlando community was entertained not only by local groups but also by popular artists from other parts of the township and the country. Colin Nxumalo recollects.

> Ooh, they used to perform, they used to perform. It was the Young Lovers, Ezami, there were the Minerals conducted by Jimmy Mojapelo the blind man, a lady by the name Thelma, there were the movers of David Thekwani, there were Beaters, 'Hot Stix' Mabuse, he was still with the Beaters, then there was Bubsy Mlangeni. Manhattan Brothers, you understand, those were the bigger groups, the likes of Letta Mbulu she was still with the Swanky Spot. We were all contemporaries, the Big Brothers, it was the Manhattan Brothers and the Pink Spots, the Woodpeckers from East Rand. Those were the kind of people we used to admire a lot. We wanted to be like them.

Growing up in Orlando West was some experience. Weekends were eagerly awaited and were times of entertainment. For young men like Colin Nxumalo, dressing in the appropriate fashion and entertaining their girlfriends came at a cost, which their parents simply could not afford. So Nxumalo and his boyhood friends spent part of their weekends doing odd jobs to earn some cash.

> *Ja*, when we grew up it was wonderful. From Standard Five up to JC (Junior Certificate) I completed school. We never used to worry our parents by then. We were a group from here in Orlando West,

every Saturday we used to go to do part-time jobs and do garden jobs [in] Greenside, Parkview. But then we used to get five shillings a day. If you were lucky you could be paid six shillings or ten shillings, then you were earning a lot of money. We came home at around five on Saturdays. Sundays we go to the *Sunday Times*, that was 44 Main Street, to insert. Help with the printing of newspapers. So we used to work the whole day, the whole night, then we knocked off in the morning the following day at five, even sometimes six o'clock, if the machine was not functioning properly. Then we come back home and sleep … but then we didn't sleep the whole Sunday because we were still energetic, we were still young boys.

> We used to dress smart, there were Paris belts, we wore Medicus shoes, and ordinary takkies but then we used to be nice also and most places that we used to buy at was at Market Street. We bought clothes only, you would just go there to fit the suit or half suit – that is a waistcoat and a trouser and a matching shirt and shoes and socks. We used to be very nice with our Dobbs caps, Aias and Smith. That is our childhood … and then our girlfriends, they also dressed nicely too, you find that you are wearing almost the same thing with your girlfriend. We wore clothes from Jeppe and Braamfontein, at the bioscope, walking by foot, doing window shopping, we used to knock off at around twelve and the bioscope starts at three … ePlanet or eMajestic or even at the Starlite. The way we grew up, very disciplined, but then there was this place where they sell alcohol. It was wine. It used to be the best wine at that time, 'Paarlpillay' then beers, milk stout and Guinness. And then we had whiskey, Black and White.

Young Sowetans prided themselves as fashion trendsetters, and few things were given as much attention as having the right look and wearing the right label. In an interview, the Mazibuko brothers expanded on this:

> It was at Lloyds, John Craig, Pakkies and Tannies, serious shops like Levisons … and we really liked Levisons then. We used to dress expensively. We would go to the church also in our expensive clothes and there was a VW car here at home and also a Chevvy Two, those old cars that accommodated us all. My father would be happy to see us all going to church at Presbyterian Church.

Gangs had terrorised communities, but they seemed to be a spent force by the early 1970s. Fashion also came and went as the seasons passed, and youths became adults. What remained a constant passion, and was the source of considerable pleasure and heartache, unity and division, was the people's game – soccer!

There can be few places in the country, and possibly the world, that experience as intense a love for soccer, and as deep a sense of rivalry, as Orlando. The location, as the home first of Orlando Pirates and then of Kaizer Chiefs, the two giants of Soweto football, was in many senses the fashion capital of the game. Owners of clubs and players were generally at the cutting edge of male fashion, but they were matched by young women, fans and partners of the players. Nokhutula Ramoitheki was at the centre of this world of glitz and glamour. In an interview, she talked about the position of young women in the local game.

> We wore black and white. To top it all I was very beautiful, very beautiful. I was Miss Junior Orlando Pirates. Yes. We had sewn skirts that were a centimetre high. The girlfriends of players like Kaizer Motaung and others were very smart. We did not wear clothes that looked like those worn by others. We showed off so that they could see that this one belonged to Chippa Moloi, this one belonged to 'Ginger Gulliver' [Kaizer Motaung]. Then their soccer kits stayed with us. You see, where it is white on a soccer boot we would clean it to outshine others, so that people could take note of who that player belonged to.
>
> When they played at Pimville sports ground, you were supposed to carry their soccer kit so that people could see you giving it to your boyfriend. The ground would be full. And the people would clap hands for you and you would then shake yourself. We used to sell Pirates badges. They cost three rands. Let's say you were given a hundred, you were supposed sell all of them. We raised funds for Pirates. These are the things we did for the Pirates.
>
> Then we wore Bakers, Saxons – the expensive shoes. We also wore the *phenduka* [reverse] skirts, the Valentines. Yes, you were supposed to show off. We had to hide our clothes from our parents. We wore them to show off, that we belonged to players like Kaizer Motaung. It was like that.

Teams were associated with particular parts of Soweto, engendering strong and enduring territorial rivalries. According to Nokhuthula,

> We only had Pirates here. And in Meadowlands, they had Meadowlands Darkies. Here we were Pirates. Swallows were from Moroka. And then there was Pimville Brothers. It was a club from Pimville. When it was a tournament, they all participated. But the club that was the opposition of Pirates was Kaizer Chiefs. Kaizer formed his own club.

Source: Bailey's African History Archive

Orlando Pirates was the dominant team in Orlando until the formation of Kaizer Chiefs

There was no doubt that Pirates was the main team in Orlando, and its matches attracted vast crowds. When the stars played, everything else had to wait. Nokhuthula continues.

> Yo! Yo! We would all go out there … kids, young, old … we would go and watch. The nice thing about it was that entrance was free. Others would stand on top of the station so that they could see. It was Pirates. We did not care that we hadn't eaten. We would rather watch Pirates instead. It was very nice, indeed. These things of fighting each other were not there, because everybody was a Pirates supporter. If you wanted to fight rather go to Pimville. It was even worse when Pirates had won the game. We would run after the losing club… [she laughs] even if you were about to get a hiding, it would be meted out later after you had returned home. Even if you had been sent to get water from Phomolong, you would leave the bucket there and go watch [Pirates], forgetting that you had been sent for water. Yes, after everything you would remember that you were supposed to get water and you had left the bucket in Phomolong, and it was no longer there. Pirates belonged here, but Kaizer split it up.

Alfred 'Russian' Jacobs was recruited to play for Orlando Pirates after impressing the club's managers during a game between the giants of Orlando and the lesser known team, Black Pirates, in which he scored a hat trick to help his team score a famous victory against their more fancied opponents. He remembers his first game for his new team:

> Just imagine that you're going to play for such a big club as Orlando Pirates and then from there you get such a huge welcome, and even end up scoring four goals. From that day till to this day that's why I said, no more going to any club. I'm staying with Pirates. And it's the truth till up to now, I'm still a Pirate.

The history of Orlando Pirates is inextricably linked with that of Orlando. Established in 1937, two years after the official creation of the location, the Orlando Pirates Boys Club was established initially to provide recreation for students and youth from the area to keep them away from anti-social activities. Sam 'Baboon' Shabangu, Bethuel Mokgosinyane and Pele Pele Mkwhanazi transformed the Boys Club into a formidable soccer team. In 1952, Orlando Pirates won every competition it entered, thereby – as Lauren Segal and Paul Holden contend in their book *Great Lives: Pivotal Moments* – establishing the team from Orlando as perhaps the leading club in the country.

In 1969, a great schism occurred in local football when a group of players, led by one of Orlando Pirates' leading stars, Kaizer Motaung, established a new club that was to create the greatest rivalry in South African soccer. According to Motaung, he found on his return from playing in the United States in 1969 that Ratha Mokgoatleng, Msomi Khoza, Zero Johnson and the late Ewert Nene had been expelled from Pirates. The official Kaizer Chiefs website proclaims that:

> There was this game between Pirates against Highlands Park which was supposed to be played in Swaziland. The trio apparently did not want to play in that game and had quarrelled with the Pirates executive. Through my contacts, I had been informed about developments while still in the States. I didn't want to interrupt anything. I simply asked Pirates permission to use the expelled players in a tour of the country to play some friendly matches. I approached Mike Tseka, then Pirates chairman and expressed fears that I foresaw trouble and suggested that perhaps it would be a perfect idea if I used the expelled players to calm down the situation as it was tense in the camp.

China Ngema, a prominent member of the Pirates club, was at the centre of events that led to the split. In an interview he has offered his views about what transpired in that fateful year of 1969:

> The three boys were suspended because they did not first get permission to go to Botswana. Pirates suspended them. Ewert took that suspension and then two days later he heard that this game was set for Swaziland [Orlando Pirates] against Highlands Park. *Hhawu*! He said to me 'How am I going to play now?' I said, I don't know. Then he said, 'I will lift the suspension of these players!' Now Ewert says, 'I will be bringing my own full squad.' They [Orlando Pirates] told him he could not do that. They told him he was just a manager, not the owner of the club. 'We are the ones who suspended these boys.' That is how the misunderstanding started. 'We're chasing you out Ewert!' they said. *Hhawu!* Our manager was being fired, only because he wanted Zero [Johnson], and the others [Ratha Mokgoatleng and Msomi Khoza] to go along to Swaziland! But we do not want to be beaten by the white boys. The white team was going to beat us in Swaziland and then laugh at us and say '*Kyk die kaffers*!' NO! We said no. That is how the split occurred. That is when Ewert was fired from the team. When Ewert left, he took a lot of people with him ... He diced to make a pick-team. We went to play around Witbank and other places, playing against other teams. We were a pick-team ...

Photograph by David Goldblatt. Courtesy of the Goodman Gallery

Cup Final, Orlando Stadium, 1972

Being booted out of what was arguably the biggest club in the country threatened to end the careers of players and managers alike. Although there was some momentum behind the group, it seemed that they were destined for the wilderness, to a 'pick-team'. But they defied the odds, and built a new team around one of Orlando Pirates' former stars, Kaizer Motaung. Ngema remembers that Kaizer's reputation, and their collective effort, laid the foundations for the emergence of another Soweto soccer giant.

> How could we not go and watch Kaizer? That was how Kaizer Chiefs was formed. We went there and watched Kaizer play with his big Afro hair. He was playing with coloureds and all the others. They played, and it was nice. Pirates then said, 'You must be mad! We are going to fire all of you!' I started the supporters' clubs. I was the one recruiting. I used my own cars. There were no cars there. They used my car. Msibi used to help me. Msibi also had a car. We struggled trying to build this team.

The creation of Kaizer Chiefs sparked huge rivalry between the teams and their supporters, especially concentrated in Orlando and surrounding parts of Soweto. China Ngema says proudly that in his part of Orlando West 'There is no Pirates supporter here. We are all Chiefs here. We are one thing'. According to Mrs Masoma, a long-standing resident of Orlando West, neighbour of China and and supporter of Kaizer Chiefs, Orlando East was the stronghold of Orlando Pirates and no one would dare walk in that area with a Kaizer Chiefs top. With some exaggeration, she claims 'If you wore Chiefs attire, they would kill you in Orlando East,' an opinion emanating from her experience:

> I was on my way home, wearing the jersey that I had bought. My home is in Orlando. I was wearing that jersey. *Jesus*, when I got to the corner of the street, I heard shouting, 'Hey you! Take off that jersey. Take off that rubbish!' I was next to my home, and then I got inside the house. They were very rough.

Although the rivalry between these two great clubs from Orlando is still very intense, the violence associated with that rivalry has gone. And then there were other local teams, apart from the major clubs. Sydney Ramokgopa and his friends spent many weekends playing the game. His family home was the headquarters of Blackhearts, which originated in Phefeni but was managed by his older brother. He played left wing for Blackhearts and he talks about how they competed. 'Orlando Callies, Mzimhlophe City Blacks … and there were others like in Meadowlands, Rangers, Zebras and so

Source: Community Collection

Dan Mashilo, local boxing star

forth. So we were playing with those teams … like the one that was giving us tough time, it was the one that other side of the mountain … Gunners.' The Reverend Papi Morris also talks about playing against teams such as 'City Ramblers, Orlando Highlanders, Kliptown Rangers, Pimville Champions, these are the teams which were tough.'

Boxing was also hugely popular among township men. Nelson Mandela was an aspiring pugilist and in his biography, *Long Walk To Freedom*, he recalls that he spent much of his free time practising at the Donaldson Orlando Community Centre. The Mazibuko brothers' father was a well-known local boxer.

> I do not know much but he used to play boxing, I remember that but I was young. He was called Blackstone and he was strong … as I am telling you … there were three of them. It was Blackstone, Punchoville and Thompson Gorrilla. Thompson Gorilla was a traffic cop under Marimba the chief of the traffic cops.

Although it was not as popular as football, boxing established itself as an important feature of young male culture in Orlando, and Soweto generally, during the 1960s. The Donaldson Orlando Community Centre had already, since the 1940s, been the mecca for boxing in Soweto. Over the years Soweto has produced some of the finest boxers – Dingaan Thobela and Baby Jake Matlala, for example – in South Africa.

■ ■ ■ ■ ■

CHAPTER SIX

WORK AND EDUCATION

'BANTU EDUCATION' WAS DESIGNED TO KEEP AFRICAN PEOPLE LOCKED in at the lower echelons of society, and was deliberately inferior to the education provided for the white population. The rationale behind the new system that was introduced from 1954 was explained by Verwoerd: 'There is no place for him [the Bantu] in the European community above the level of certain forms of labour'. The new education system was part of the state's broader strategy to bring Africans under control but it had one advantage in that the number of African students in schools increased significantly. In Soweto, as we have seen, this was especially noticeable in the high proportion of children in primary schools.

In the 1960s, the state stopped building schools in Soweto and the result was endemic overcrowding. The average pupil:teacher ratios increased to 58:1 in 1967 from an already high 46:1 at the time Bantu Education was introduced. The quality of education was also severely undermined by the large numbers of unqualified and under-qualified teachers – it was estimated that in 1961 fewer than ten per cent of African teachers had a matric certificate. Not surprisingly, the students suffered. Between 1948 and 1968 the matric pass rate declined from fifty-four per cent to thirty-three per cent.

Despite such impediments, and even though schooling was not compulsory for African children, the Orlando community placed a high premium on education. Parents generally attempted, under very trying

Seventh Day Adventist School

Source: Community Collection

economic circumstances to keep their children in school for as long as possible. They were supported by some deeply committed educationists, such as Thamsanqa Khambule and Lungiswa Bacela, and many others.

Lungiswa Bacela has told her story in an interview. It reflects the centrality of education in her own life and her dedication to the education of young people in Soweto. She started her schooling in Pimville and when her grandmother moved to Orlando she joined her and went to school 'under the late Jolobe of the Presbyterian school. I was also taught by Mr Maseko, who was the principal there, next to Orlando Stadium. That is where I finished my Standard Six.' At that time African women had very limited employment options. Those who had the opportunity to study beyond the first phase of schooling often chose either nursing or teaching, professions that carried prestige in the community. As Mrs Bacela explains, she had her heart set on becoming a nurse.

> I went to continue with my education in Bethel [in 1945], in the Eastern Cape. My interest has always been to do nursing, but the school had no interest in nursing any more. And I switched to teaching. I did teaching, and I completed in 1949.

With a teaching qualification, Mrs Bacela immediately returned to Orlando West, where in January 1950 she opened the Orlando West School, which became known as the Seventh-Day Adventist School in the street now named after her, Bacela Street. Her enthusiasm for the profession made an immediate impact. She recalls that a growing number of parents wanted to send their children to her school.

> There were many of them. So many that it became a problem with the other schools like Holy Cross, where Mr Bhele was the principal. He thought that I was going to take children from his school. It was a miracle because my school was talked about a lot. One of my brothers left Holy Cross to come to my school while the other one remained. Our school was up to Standard Four then. Yes, it started from Sub A.
>
> So after children had finished with us, the parents wanted to know why they were leaving the school and we told them that we only went up to Standard Four. Our pupils were getting the best education. I am not boasting here.

The school's success came to the attention of the state school authorities, especially the local inspectors.

> The inspector during that time was Gugushe Nomawushe. I remember one day as they were begging us, because of good progress from our school. They were begging us to leave that school and join the government schools, but we told them we were working for the church. We even told them we were satisfied there. They told us that they would give us better remuneration and we told them that our reward is from heaven. She told me that there were problems in other schools, the teachers do not teach but instead open tuck shops in the school premises for our children to buy on debt. And that was one of the things that made us different. I also remember one day when Gugushe came to my class while I was teaching, she told me that I was doing well. People could see the difference between learners who were from other schools and those who had not developed with us.

Colin Nxumalo began his schooling in the 1940s, when his parent sent him to a crèche in Orlando West. 'There was a house that was used as a crèche venue, DR Rathebe's house. I went to that crèche, until I went to primary school. I went to Holy Cross primary school.' At this point his education was affected by the introduction of Bantu Education. He recalls the dramatic changes that occurred.

Orlando West School

Photograph by Sally Gaule

> I went to the Holy Cross until 1955. That was the time of Bantu Education. They changed Holy Cross to Bhele Community School. By then they were changing most of the things. The schools were being divided according to ethnicity, the Zulu speaking were supposed to be on their own, the same goes with the Sotho, the Tsonga. We were then removed from Bhele, because we were the Zulu speaking. We were then taken to Mooki Memorial in Orlando East, that was 1955.

Shirley Thathi's early school career was severely disrupted by the state's insistence on the ethnic segregation of schools.

> I started my schooling at Mzamo [Lower Primary]. You know, my mother's father is a Xhosa, so we knew Xhosa when we were growing up, and Mzamo Primary School was a school for Xhosas only. And that is where we went. And then later my mother learned isiZulu and she failed to help us with homework. And that is why we ended up coming to Thloreng [Lower Primary], and then she was able to help us with our homework. When we finished at Thloreng, the teachers used to evaluate us somehow, I am not sure of the criteria used, because the teachers used to tell us where to go after finishing here at Thloreng between Bhele or Thulasizwe [Higher Primaries]. We even thought that, maybe, they used to look at who stays near Phomolong, so that they could go to a nearby school, next to the side in which they resided. So, I was told to go to Thulasizwe.

Source: Community Collection

Dutch Reformed Church: Churches had a significant presence in the township

The situation was better in the few high schools. Colin Nxumalo benefited from attending Mr Khambule's school. However, the introduction and building of new high schools in Orlando West presented new challenges to students and teachers.

> I then went to Orlando High in 1957. Our principal then was Thamsanqa Khambule. We were at Orlando High, many young people from Orlando West, up to end of 1957. When they started Orlando West Secondary school in 1958, the school then moved from Orlando, to Orlando West just next to my home. When the school moved from Orlando West, they found that in Orlando West we were going to do form two. I think I did my form two, I stayed for some few months at Bhele which is inside the premises of Orlando West Secondary school. By then we were under Dr Matseke then in 1958 or 1959 Orlando West started to operate, they finished building it, we then moved to Orlando West to do our junior certificate ... after I completed my JC, I then left because I had siblings.

Wilfred Thabethe also began his schooling before Bantu Education.

> 'I started my schooling at Mooki school', he explains, 'It was a missionary school, was built by the church mission in England. I finished my higher primary school at the Methodist. Now it is called Ematsheni. It was still a missionary school by the Methodist Church. Then

I moved to Orlando High School. It was named Raboroko. The name is now is Lakeng, but it is Orlando High School. So I stayed there for three years, and obtained my junior certificate.

Many students of that the time remember their teachers as dedicated, and were profoundly influenced by them. Sydney Ramokgopa was in primary school in the 1960s and firmly believes that teachers at the school played a major role in his development.

> Firstly let me say that the outstanding teacher to me it was Mrs Ledwaba. I mean, that is the teacher who taught me to read and write at a primary level … the most important teacher is the one who taught you how to read and write.
>
> So at high school level then you are already at a certain stage, well at high school at Morris Isaacson, I think we had really outstanding teachers. First and foremost, the major one, our principal, Mr Mathabathe, he could understand what was happening in the school. And even some of the teachers. They could understand the students. So they were very, very outstanding, because I remember one of our teachers that was Abram Tiro, who was expelled from Turfloop, he was teaching us History, but at a certain point he would deviate, tell us about, you know, the material conditions of the society, what was really happening.

In the early 1970s, the state built several additional schools in Soweto. Thami Zitha started secondary school during this period and remembers that

> a lot of people managed to finish school … you were lucky if your parents managed to get you to secondary until you obtained your Form Five. But the rest who could not and only had Standard Six were able to get a decent job. But after finishing my Standard Six I went to Dube at Daliwonga Secondary to do the rest of my high school until 1975. I got 'i-cover' [sponsorship], which sent me to boarding school because I was accepted.

But with this increase in high schools in the early 1970s all sorts of problems, some of which had been present before, were exacerbated. Corporal punishment was endemic in the education system as teachers, who were often badly qualified and lacked basic pedagogic skills, used forced to impose control over students. Although Shirley Thathi thinks the teachers 'were all right', regular punishment at their hands left a deep impression on her.

> There was this corporal punishment then, where we were beaten with a cane stick that they used to soak in water to retain shape. We would come back home with marks on our backs. They would punish us if, for example, we did not do handwork. If you did not finish your hemming stitch, or whatever in sewing. We would be punished even if we did not complete homework. A teacher would throw your book out through the window and it will fall into pieces. It was difficult then. Before teachers arrived in the morning, they should find us in a queue, singing memory verses like 'Nkulunkulu' [God] and others, I just forget them. But teachers should find us waiting for them, singing. If a teacher found us not singing, they would beat us. It made us feel bad, it was very painful. I had a case where I was beaten to the extent that my parents were involved. I was beaten by a female teacher, who used to teach us sewing, and my parents got involved.

South Africa experienced unprecedented economic growth in the 1960s – between seven per cent and nine per cent in the latter half of the decade After the initial flight of capital following the Sharpeville massacre, multinational companies invested heavily in the country. A high demand for labour tended to push up African wages, although they continued to lag far behind those of whites. However, apartheid severely restricted the possibilities of upward mobility for African people and as a result most were confined to unskilled and semi-skilled employment. Mrs Mafafane, who qualified as a teacher, remembers that many of her female neighbours were employed in low-wage jobs.

> So they would bring the laundry to their houses, wash and iron them, then take it back to the owners when done. Yes, that's how they used to live. Then other people were factory workers. Yes, the job was there, enough for everybody. There were no mine workers, just the locals.

Nokuthula Ramoitheki was forced to leave school after she fell pregnant and found it difficult to get employment. 'It was not easy', she says. 'Your mother would assist you in finding a job. For example, if your mother worked at a factory she would request for you to be employed there, like doing small things such as taking off cotton using scissors, or whatever you could do. It was not easy.' She eventually secured permanent employment in a factory in George Goch because her mother and aunt worked there. 'My job was to glue the bags inside and put the lining inside.' For this she earned a mere two pounds ten shillings. But, '… it was a lot. You could lay-by an expensive jersey, and the following week pay it off.' Wilfred Thabethe also started working at a factory after leaving school. 'I started to work in the factory in Doornfontein. Like many Sowetans with a measure of formal education, he was not employed as a manual worker. 'My first employment', he recalls, 'was as a clerk at the factory. As a dispatch clerk at the factory for five years. I used to enjoy it there, I used to call it the greener pastures. They really paid me. The greener pastures is that I worked for seventy rands a week … seventy rands per week was very pleasing … it was a lot of money a week.'

There were fewer employment opportunities available to African women who completed high school and had post-school qualifications. Most, like the notable examples Albertina Sisulu, Winnie Mandela and Lungiswa Bacela became nurses, social workers or teachers. Shirley Thathi's grandmother worked as an assistant nurse at Baragwanath Hospital, while her mother was employed at the OK Bazaars Warehouse in the city.

The massive expansion of Johannesburg from the 1950s, which accelerated further during the economic boom of the 1960s, created new job opportunities in retail, service and banking for Soweto's population. Thami Zitha's recollection of his mother's employment suggests that workers were even able to improve their employment status over time.

> My mother was working at Snappers. At Snappers they were selling school uniforms, it was a school uniform shop … [she then moved] … if I remember quite properly, in that administration she worked in the draughtsman department, where they drafted plans. Housing plans. That place closed down, and she moved and worked for a bank, Nedbank … Mum worked in and out of Nedbank until she retired, working for the housing division.

Zitha's father worked at an advertising company, J Walker Thomson, until he was able to buy a house in Port Elizabeth. Sydney Ramokgopa's father worked at the same company, John Orr's, nearly all his working life of thirty years, while his mother was a domestic worker. Colin Nxumalo became a member of the municipal police in 1960, which, in his words, 'was the end of my youth'. He was stationed at the municipal offices in Dube and remembers that as a young man he was forced to start at the bottom of the employment ladder. 'Back then when you wanted to work for the municipality, you first started to work as a labourer … if you wanted to be a clerk, you started there, as a labourer, irrespective of your qualifications.' He was fired from this job for missing work. 'I started at the time when the Easter holidays were near. I went to a picnic only to find out that on the same weekend I am supposed to report for work.' He quickly found employment as a 'messenger boy' at a shop. Fortunately for him, a colleague's father found out that he had qualifications and managed to arrange employment as a police clerk at the Selby hostel. Within a few years he succeeded in becoming a traffic officer in Soweto.

Some occupations, such as teaching and nursing, held significant status in the community because they signified membership of an educated elite. Lungiswa Bacela says that '... the only people that used to have better jobs that I still remember were Mr Monathebe, who was a teacher at the Methodist Church School, people like Mr Xorile. Those were recognised men.' And Mrs Mafafane continues to get recognition many years after she retired from the teaching profession. 'Up to now they are still calling me teacher. I have always earned their respect, even their children call me teacher all these years. And they used to call my husband *ntate titjhere.*'

■ ■ ■ ■ ■

CHAPTER SEVEN

INSPIRED BY BLACK CONSCIOUSNESS

STATE REPRESSION IN THE 1960S STRUCK DEBILITATING BLOWS AGAINST the liberation movements. In comparison to the campaigns of the 1950s and the intense political struggles that followed the 16 June uprising, the sixties could be described as a period of political quiescence. Such a general description tends to obscure the presence of political opposition, albeit often individualised and short-lived opposition that had only limited impact on the apartheid state. But even when, in the late 1960s and early 1970s, apartheid appeared all-powerful, there were already signs of a new mood of defiance, with the youth of the townships playing a leading role.

An early example of efforts by a new generation of political activists to link up with older activists occurred in the late 1960s and was centred on Orlando West and Diepkloof. A number of key activists who were involved in the Congress Movement, and especially in the trade unions, reached out to younger activists with the aim of re-establishing some semblance of a political presence in the township. Winnie Mandela, Rita and Lawrence Ndzinga, Samson Ndou and Joyce Sikhakhane were some of the people involved. Snuki Zikalala, who lived in Diepkloof and attended school in Orlando, was drawn into this informal network by Winnie Mandela in 1966 or 1967. Others who worked with Zikalala were George Mokwebo and Daniel Tsotetsi, both from Diepkloof, and Joseph Stimulo Banda from Orlando. Over the next few months the older activists attempted to provide these young people with basic political education. Snuki Zikalala was to say:

> Joyce [Sikhakhane] gave us ANC politics. Then in the second week we organised another meeting at my place. What she did, she brought Samson Ndou. He also came and gave us ... ANC politics. Then they introduced adult people from the ANC. The other one was Lawrence Ndzinga from Dube. He came and gave us a lecture about the ANC then he started giving us Marxist literature and ANC literature and then we started reading about the struggle itself. But now what frustrated us was there was no action, it was politics, politics.

After months of political education, Zikalala and his comrades began to recruit more young people from Orlando and Diepkloof. The network began to adopt a more formal structure, with cells consisting of between five and ten people each, and soon it extended its operations to other parts of Soweto and the country. Snuki estimates that at its height in 1969 there were about 300 people involved. But this growth also brought the network to the attention of the security police, who detained many of its leading members in May 1969, and charged them under the Terrorism Act. Although they were acquitted, the state continued to hold a number of them in solitary confinement for several months. State repression may have crushed this attempt to rekindle an internal underground organisation, but it certainly did not succeed in halting the mushrooming of opposition ideas among the youth.

Source: Wits Historical Papers

Steve Biko, founder of Black Conciousness

It may not have been the only reason, but the main reason for the new mood of defiance among young people was the emergence of the Black Consciousness Movement. In the late 1960s, black students grew increasingly dissatisfied with the absence of a black student body that could represent their interests at universities. At white universities, progressive black students participated in the National Union of South African Students, or Nusas, which was dominated by white students. Steve Biko, who had emerged as the leading intellectual of Black Consciousness and was a stridently defiant voice for black students, led his comrades out of Nusas, with the intention of establishing a new, all-black student organisation. In 1969 Biko and his comrades, including Barney Pityana and Strini Moodley, officially launched the South African Students' Organisation, SASO. The manifesto of the new organisation articulated some of the core principles of Black Consciousness: an attitude of mind, a way of life. 'The basic tenet of Black Consciousness is that the Blackman must reject all value systems that seek to make him a foreigner in the country of his birth and reduce his basic dignity,' and 'The Blackman must build up his own value system, see himself as self-defined and not as defined by others.'

These were powerful ideas that resonated with large sections of township youth, especially those who were educated. Within a few years SASO had

Source: Bailey's African History Archive

ABOVE:
The Black People's Convention was established in the early 1970s

established a strong presence on university campuses across the country, particularly at the black only institutions, and by the early 1970s the Black Consciousness Movement had launched the Black People's Convention and the South African Students' Movement, SASM, to organise secondary school students. SASM relatively quickly established a strong presence in the secondary schools of Orlando, inspiring the emergence of a new generation of activists. Sydney Ramokgopa has told of how the organisation grew in Orlando:

> SASM was now gaining momentum particularly in the secondary schools and the high schools. And then in Morris Isaacson, we had our own structure there. William Nkonyeli, Amos Masondo, Murphy Morobe, Billy Masetlha and so forth, they were so many. So we came together and then we formed SASM that was really based in Soweto, and then others they joined us like Sekanontaone, Orlando High, Orlando West and so forth.

Orlando High and Orlando West were strong SASM branches, arguably the strongest in the country. Many activists of the time ascribe the spread of Black Consciousness ideas and the growth of SASM to the influence of progressive young teachers, especially teachers of History. Onkgopotse Abram Tiro was perhaps the best known of these teacher activists. He rose to prominence when he delivered a scathing attack against the apartheid system at a graduation ceremony at the University of the North, colloquially known as 'Turfloop'. The authorities expelled him, triggering a massive strike on the campus. He was then employed as a History teacher at Morris Isaacson – albeit for only six months before the authorities again removed him from his position. Nonetheless, his brief stint at the school is generally remembered as a key moment in the political awakening of many students.

Sydney Ramokgopa also recalls another History teacher, Ralph Manyane, introducing 'topics that really involve the lives and the society in general'. The early 1970s was a time of political exploration, search for radical ideologies, developing critiques of apartheid and capitalism, and trying to work out how to overcome the system. It was an exciting time as young people began rebuilding the internal liberation movement, step by step. All over Soweto young activists were busy forming small groups – discussion circles, reading groups, debating societies – to grapple with radical ideologies and to organise themselves. A number of these groups operated in Orlando, and involved students from the secondary schools. Patrick Sekuthi describes how concerns among some friends over the undemocratic appointment of prefects led to the formation of one such group.

> We sat together with Willy Nkonyela and Raymond Pilane, then just debating topics that … we need to do something about the system here at school. We are not so much happy about the way things are … the administration of the school is forcing these prefects on us, now we need to chase this system, move away from where prefects would be chosen by the administration, we as students, we should be in a position to choose our own prefects. So we roped in Sydney Ramokgopa, then we roped in Oupa Motlana … we started having meetings.

But before they could proceed to formulate a clear position and start to mobilise their fellow students, the principal got wind of the fact that they were meeting regularly.

> I don't know how this ended up in the principal's office, it came to his ear that these guys, this is their intention, they normally hold meetings, you know, when we are supposed to be in class, so they got

> to change the system. The police were called and they suspended us. He said, if you want to come back you must bring along your parents.

The principal of Morris Isaacson at the time was a Mr Mathabathe, who was evidently nervous about what appeared to be the start of political mobilisation at his school. And if Patrick Sekuthi and his comrades expected any sympathy from their parents they were mistaken. When he arrived with his mother at the school, the principal reiterated the administration's policy regarding the appointment of prefects and told them that elections by students only happened at universities, so they would have to wait. If they did not agree to this they should go home with their parents, 'or go try their luck somewhere else'. Patrick's mother's response was typical of the parents:

Protesting students at Morris Isaacson in the early 1970s

> So, well, my mom said, 'Now look, Mr Mathabathe, this is my son and as soon as he leaves this gate he stops to be my son, as soon as he reaches Morris Isaacson school gates and he enters those gates, he is your son, when he moves out from those gates he stops being my son and he ends up being your own son, so he's your responsibility.'.

This exposed an important and deep cleavage between the youth and their parents. Thami Zitha's view on this is that, 'during the 1960s our parents were afraid to talk about politics, because if they did they were going to be arrested. People did not trust each other.'

Sydney Ramokgopa has a more critical opinion. 'Our parents, they were mostly very conservative.'

> I remember one time, we met one old man there, and this old man he said, 'You will end up just like,' he even said, 'just like that fool Mothopeng.' Mothopeng was speaking openly, he didn't fear anything. Most of the parents they were really conservative, they didn't want [us to be like] Zephania Mothopeng. And they will always want to watch their children, what they are doing.

Sydney Ramokgopa came from a political family. Both his parents were aligned to the ANC in the 1950s, and his father was probably a member. His older brother was also a member, and went into exile in 1963, which resulted in regular harassment from the security police. Perhaps it was due to this direct experience with the state's security forces that Ramokgopa's parents were nervous about the prospect of their younger son also becoming involved in anti-apartheid politics.

> The politics of that old generation is that they were not open. Now the new generation it was open, and we saw what was happening. Like for instance when you look at the statement that Tiro made during the convocation in Turfloop, he was very open and clear. So, really, in our parents during that time there was, let us say, that fear of the system.

Sydney Ramagkgopa in exile in Botswana

At the time Sekuthi's and Ramokgopa's group was uncovered in 1974 they had been politically active for three years,as individual members of national organisations. Ramokgopa's evolution as a political activist mirrors the experiences of many of his generation.

> I think around 1971 when I was at Morris Isaacson there was a certain Simon Radebe, he was a member of Nayo [National Youth Organisation]. So we joined. Then a lot of students joined. In 1972, I think, there was a conference in Hammanskraal. Now this conference was called by the South African Student Organisation, as well as the Black People's Convention ... that is where even the constitution of SASO was changed. We had to have students, particularly in the secondary school, where they would have their own organisation. So, from that conference, that is where SASM came in.

By 1973 and 1974 a new mood of activism had developed among the youth of Orlando. This was reflected not only in the growth of discussion groups and formal organisations, but also in the burgeoning protest theatre, much of which took place at Uncle Tom's Hall. Patrick Sekuthi remembers that 'around that period, you know, there were plays, so we used to go there to watch those, they stimulated us, you know'. *Sizwe Banzi Is Dead*, the iconic play with John Kani in the lead, resonated with the anger felt by a growing number of young black people. Patrick's words capture the power of the play.

> We were already politically minded and when we were exposed to such plays, where we could see this gentleman acting a part of a father who is being harassed by a teenager white police boy harassing him and then taking off his hat and squeezing that hat ... and when you know at home, when your dad comes in he takes off the hat and he holds that hat, tidily and so on, it's your dad's hat ... from work. You feel proud about your dad, and you are the one who has to put that hat safely away somewhere and now it's been crackly squeezed and that. Now he was holding an orange, symbolising a hat, and then squeezing that orange. You know, it affected us, it touched us, and

> that really conscientised us and made us aware … a black man's life really is worthless.

The political mood was changing in the townships. One of the important shifts that took place in the early 1970s was that a small but growing number of township students were committing themselves to the struggle for freedom. They came to the conclusion that radical ideas, sacrifice and organisation would be required to achieve their goals. This marked the beginning of a decisive break with the political lull of the post-Sharpeville period, when political organisations were banned, leaders were imprisoned for long periods and widespread repression instilled fear in large sections of the population. Sekuthi, Ramokgopa and their comrades reflected the political sea change underway at the time. After their experience with the principal and the authorities, the group now took the critical decision to change its *modus operandi.* They realised that it was still too easy for 'the system' to isolate and silence critics. 'We sat down and figured out, we said, guys, you see this SASM thing is going to put us in trouble. [If we talk openly about this now] we will be easily victimised, silenced, things like that.'

The group came to the decisive conclusion that it should 'try to operate, go underground. We decided, now what we are going to do, we are going to operate as closed units, and call those unit cells.' Sekuthi tells of what they did next.

> Then we formed a Soweto Seven. It was myself, Sydney Ramokgopa, Oupa Motlana, Raymond Pilane, Amos Masondo, Joe the elderly guy, Roy Masinga. We assigned duties to each other. And then first it was we are going to split, but not necessarily split, but one has to go out and organise four people and form a cell, and then another one would be introduced … So we spread like that … so we had a mother body and we would sit down and we would now come up with policies, decide what to do, what not to do … And we said we need to organise literature to politicise ourselves and then this literature – more especially banned literature – started to go to the other cells.

It's not clear how much success the 'Soweto Seven' had in spreading their underground network. One of the first things they did was to organise a trip to Botswana, to get a sense of the political movements in exile, and to get more banned literature. Here they met Clarence Hamilton, who was a member of a semi-clandestine network based in the neighbouring Noordgesig. After their return to Orlando the group again came to the attention of the security police, which led to the arrest and subsequent torturing of Amos Masondo. At this point, several members including

Sekuthi and Ramokgopa decided to go into exile to avoid imprisonment. Their decision to skip the country coincided with reports of more open protests by students directed primarily against the state's decision to impose Afrikaans as a medium of instruction in all African schools.

■ ■ ■ ■ ■

CHAPTER EIGHT

THE BEGINNING OF THE UPRISING

BETWEEN 1972 AND 1975 SCHOOLING IN SOWETO WAS DRAMATICALLY transformed. Under pressure from industrialists who desperately required more black labour, especially in semi-skilled jobs, the state reversed its policy of not building schools in urban townships, and during this period forty new schools were built in Soweto, including a number of secondary schools. As a consequence the student population increased exponentially over a very short space of time – in the late 1960s the number of students in Soweto was estimated at about 90 000 but in 1976 that figure had increased to 170 000. Significantly, the number of secondary school students registered an even more spectacular rate of growth, from 12 656 in 1974 to 34 656 in 1976. However, just as the demand for schooling increased, state investment in urban African education dropped dramatically again from about 1974. In fact, there was a stark racially-based inequality in state expenditure on education: R644 per white student compared to a mere R42 per African child, with Soweto parents having to pay school fees of R102 a year. Massive overcrowding in schools, particularly in the entry level of secondary school, reached crisis proportions in 1976, and inevitably added to the growing discontent among secondary school students.

Conditions in the township were deteriorating. Even as the population of Soweto grew, the provision of public housing declined sharply. According to the historian Clive Glaser, between 1966 and 1969 the state built fewer than 2000 new houses in Soweto. By the early 1970s the extent of the mounting housing crisis in Soweto became apparent. An industry survey found in 1970 that an average of thirteen people lived in each 'match-box' house in the township, and five years later that figure had increased to seventeen. Moreover, only fourteen per cent of households had electricity and a meager three per cent had access to hot water. This, too, contributed to the anger felt by an increasing number of township residents towards the apartheid system. There was a growing list of grievances but not yet a single issue around which a general campaign could coalesce and which activists could use to mobilise in schools and the broader community.

Then, government's universally decried decision to impose Afrikaans provided a central focus around which activists could campaign. According to the historian Sifiso Ndlovu, the Afrikaaner Broederbond had been driving an agenda to promote Afrikaans among African people from the late 1960s, with a view to countering the growing influence of English and undermining the possibility of critical thinking among African school pupils. It was not surprising then that the thought of having to be taught in Afrikaans generated such immediate and widespread anger. Within months of the announcement by the minister of Bantu education and development, MC Botha, opposition was voiced publicly. Teachers at Phefeni Junior Secondary signed a petition because, as they said, there was 'no way' they could do it. In early January 1975, the African Teachers' Association of South Africa, Atasa, sent a memorandum to the Department of Bantu Education asking it to reconsider its decision and to take into account the views of African people. But the Department was adamant. It would continue with its policy. In his address to the National Assembly in May 1975, Punt Janson, the deputy minister, was characteristically unapologetic about the government's approach on this matter: '

> No, I have not consulted the African people on the language issue and I'm not going to. I have consulted the Constitution of the Republic of South Africa. ... The leaders of the various homelands can in due course decide what they want to do in their own homelands where they are the masters. However, as far as the white areas are concerned this is a decision that has been taken and I am going to stand by it.

Such disdain caused even the usually moderate Atasa to step up its campaign against Afrikaans. The extent of the anger was also reflected in an editorial in *The World*, on 6 January 1975:

> Why should we in the urban areas have Afrikaans – a language spoken nowhere else in the world and which is still in a raw state of de-

> velopment, in any case – pushed down our throats? The implications of this new directive are too serious to leave now. We urge parents to join forces with teachers all over the country and fight the directive. The government must be left in no doubt at all about how seriously we view their highhanded action … The situation can only deteriorate further unless the new regulations are scrapped.

Further attempts to persuade the authorities to change their minds continued over the next year, but it was all to no avail. Students also voiced their opposition, mainly in meetings and discussions. However, opposition to Afrikaans remained rather uneven, as no one really knew what impact it would have on education. This was to change very quickly when the new system was implemented at the start of the academic year in January 1976. Most African teachers could simply not teach in Afrikaans. Jon-Jon Mkhonza explained the disastrous consequences to the authors of *Soweto – A History*.

> There was one teacher by the name of Mr Modisane. He was teaching Afrikaans, History and Mathematics, so we told him that we didn't understand this language; couldn't he explain in English? He said, 'No.' So … I mean … we couldn't understand. Just imagine from March until, I think it was in May, we were still blank on those subjects.

Mrs Sithole, who started teaching in Soweto the year that Bantu Education was introduced, has confirmed that most teachers found it extremely difficult to teach in Afrikaans. 'To be honest, Afrikaans was also a problem even to us teachers. Just imagine teaching Mathematics in Afrikaans. That was totally insane. We couldn't do it. We would laugh about it and crack jokes like, come let us count, *een, twee, drie*.' She laughed. 'What do you call plus in Afrikaans?'

All schools faced the same problem. Anger among students rose. In May, Orlando West (Phefeni Junior Secondary School) became the site of the first major demonstration against Afrikaans. Until then demonstrations were isolated and short-lived. On 18 May 1976, *The World* reported that 600 students at the school went on strike to demand the scrapping of Afrikaans.

> Students threatened to beat up their headmaster and threw [Afrikaans] textbooks out of classroom windows in a demonstration against being taught some subjects in Afrikaans. The 600 students from Phefeni Junior Secondary School, Orlando West, then went on strike and refused to attend any classes. In a violent display of pupil-power yesterday the students also demanded the re-instatement of Mr Mahlangu, chairman of the school board, whom they

Source: South African Historical Archive (SAHA)

Soweto students reject Afrikaans

> claimed had been sacked because he was against using Afrikaans for teaching. The demonstration started after the morning assembly when students from Form One and Form Two refused to go to their classrooms … Some let down the tyres of the principal's car. They then confronted the principal, Mr SC Mpulo, and demanded that he call the school inspector. They said the inspector should come and explain why difficult subjects were taught in Afrikaans.

A similar demonstration, attempted at Naledi High, turned into a confrontation between students and the police. Between 17 and 24 May several schools from Orlando East, Pimville and Diepkloof embarked on a boycott. It was evident that students' anger was boiling over and they were becoming more determined to mount direct action. From mid-May to mid-June, student organisations, notably SASM and other political organisations, worked feverishly to coordinate the struggle against Afrikaans. The SASM conference of 28 May came out in strong support of the student boycott, and thereafter SASM linked up with the local coordinating committee that appeared to be behind some of the class boycotts, including with one of the emerging student leaders, Seth Mazibuko. Sibongile Mkhabela, a student at Naledi High, remembers the first two weeks of June being characterised by 'serious mobilisation in the schools … mainly through SASM. SASM members were saying that this situation could not be allowed to continue. That was the build up to the meeting on June 13th.' Seth Mazibuko's testimony in 1977 at the trial against him and other student leaders for organising the 1976 demonstrations, offers an insight into what transpired at that meeting.

> Various schools of Soweto were present at this meeting … there was a large attendance … The main speaker was a man called Aubrey who explained to us what the aims and objects of SASM were. He also discussed the use of Afrikaans as a means of tuition or language and called upon the prefects of our schools to come forward and to explain what the position was there. I stood up and told the congregation that the Phefeni School refused to use Afrikaans and they had boycotted classes during May 1976. Aubrey then enquired how could other schools support us in our stand as they were writing exams and Phefeni was not … Aubrey then asked for suggestions from the floor. Don [Tsietsi] Mashinini suggested that a mass demonstration should be held on 16.6.76 by all black schools … The election for the new [Soweto region] committee for SASM was then held. Aubrey also explained that all prefects and the monitors would be formed into an Action Committee.

On 15 June the Action Committee met again, to make the final arrangements for the mass peaceful demonstration the following day. It was a day that would not only change South Africa forever. It would also etch Orlando into the minds of many people across the world as the place where the uprising that eventually overthrew apartheid started.

The Action Committee's plan was clear: students would march from different schools, pass through Orlando West via Phefeni School (to demonstrate solidarity with the students who had boycotted classes) and then gather at the Orlando stadium, from where they would march to the regional offices of the Department of Education to hand over a memorandum of their demands. Along the way, students went from school to school calling on those who were still in class to join the march. Mrs Mafafane, a teacher at Kgotso Lower Primary, did not object to teaching Afrikaans and was opposed to student boycotts. She recalls what happened at her school on the morning of 16 June.

> Yes, we were at school. I remember I was even teaching Afrikaans, *bo, ka, was* … Then somebody came running and told me, 'Hey Mistress! Look there by the Sekanontwane passage!' There were lots of people coming from that side, they didn't care whether you were busy teaching, they knock and say 'OUT! You are teaching Afrikaans?' I said, 'What does Afrikaans do? And they said 'Ma'am, OUT! Stop this, we don't want it, release these children now! Then we all went out, we sat outside.

Colin Nxumalo was on traffic duty that morning, on the Nancefield-Moroka Road.

> I was working with this other friend of mine, a traffic officer, Fraser Ramokgopha. In the morning we saw a group of schoolchildren, they were coming from that side of crossroads, coming towards us, we were standing at the intersection, at Mncube and Nancefield. They were coming down Nancefield-Moroka Road. As they were coming, they closed the road and filled the street, so we went to them, trying to control the traffic, because it was still in the morning, and taxis were on the road going to the Nancefield station. We tried to control traffic and also to ensure that they were safe. We took these children, we took them I think few metres away from the intersection. They then came to the intersection, Mncube Drive, they were going to turn at Mncube Drive. We are going to Orlando West, we are going to meet other students at Orlando West …

Photograph by Peter Magubane. Courtesy SAHA

Students and police clash in Soweto

Once the students reached Orlando West, the situation changed dramatically as the police attempted to stop the march with violence. According to Nxumalo they had tried to do this earlier,

> Then as we were at the corner, there came 41 hundred [Chevrolet 4100] one is cream-white and the other one is green. I will never forget that … those Chevs 41 hundred, we know them after all, that they are the security cars. They then started shooting and pouring teargas, only to find out that teargas was not effective. They started at Mncube and Nancefield Moroka, they started there to pour teargas. Those teargases were not effective … I think they have noticed that this thing is useless, we thought they gave up, but only to find out that they were going to reinforce, apparently.

Mrs Sithole watched the students as they marched down the road.

> Yes! I said, this is now serious, and they're now at school, and now they came down, now they were singing. As I went out, I saw police at the corner, at the robot … they were standing there. I said to myself, No! They won't do anything. The children came, and they came down this way, coming down, thousands … thousands of them, thousands all in school uniform. They had nothing, they were not aggressive. They just had placards saying 'Away with Afrikaans'.

Mrs Sithole says that what happened next is still embedded in her mind.

> When the police came … I was outside watching. Now I'm worried, where are these kids? Because now I can see the police vans and everything. When they were just near here the police came and they talked, saying to them 'go back to school' and children said 'NO!' They were against Afrikaans. They did not have stones, they didn't have anything! Whoever said the children had anything like stones? It's not so, it's a lie. The police just opened fire. There were little children coming from this side. They came from this street. I remember their uniform was green and grey. They came from this side and the police opened fire! And all hell broke loose here. And the little boy fell here, between these two houses, between my house and here…

The police shot indiscriminately into the mass of students. The killings of Hastings Ndlovu and Hector Pieterson have come to symbolise the violence of the apartheid security forces. Sifiso Ndlovu, who has written some of the most vivid accounts and perceptive analyses of the uprising, explains that Hastings Ndlovu had led a group of students who were planning to march from Orlando West Junior Secondary to Orlando Stadium. They were confronted by police at the Orlando West bridge where Hastings was shot at close range by Colonel Kleingeld. Hector Pieterson's death and the picture taken by Sam Nzima of Mbuyisa Makhubo carrying Pieterson's lifeless body with Antoinette Sithole, Pieterson's sister, running alongside, became the iconic moment and image of the 1976 uprising. Sifiso Ndlovu has recorded how Antoinette has vividly recounted the dramatic moments of her brother's shooting by the police.

> As we came out from hiding, I was scared and I said: 'It seems this is going to go on and on. So what can one do?' I was thinking very hard and I forgot about Hector … We came on foot. That's another problem. Even if you want to go home, how are you going to go home? So I was thinking about that … I looked around, thinking maybe he's still hiding. He's small. Maybe he's still hiding, he's still frightened … I told myself that I'm not going to move from that place. He might come looking for me. Let me stay here. While I was there, thinking about that, I could see a group of boys, about three or four, at a distance … They were struggling and other students who were hanging around on the pavement were going to that scene … I want to go there but I don't know how because I'm thinking of Hector, that he might look for me and not find me … I was very scared. It's almost about seven minutes and Hector hasn't come out. My heart was beating so fast but I tried to get hold of myself. As they came closer, the gentleman … whom I knew later [as] Mbuyisa Makhubo … lifted … a body and, as he lifted it higher, the first thing that I saw was the front part of Hector's shoe. Then I said: 'Those shoes belong to Hector!' I just said that and I just went to the scene. Mbuyisa was already running. And on the way when we were running I asked him: 'Who are you? This is my brother, I've been looking for him.' I didn't know how to explain myself.

The police killed more than a hundred people and injured many more in three bloody days of violent repression against students. Students reacted angrily and battled the heavily armed police with stones. Within days the revolt spread to Alexandra township, where the police exacted bloody revenge on the population, to the East Rand, and then to other parts of the country.

In Soweto, the students' struggle became more organised and consciously reached out to parents and workers for support. At the beginning of August, the Soweto Student Representative Council, or SSRC, was created, to better coordinate the struggles. Tsietsi Mashinini was elected as its first chairman. Three stayaways were organised, in August and September, as students attempted to build an alliance with workers in support of their demands. These actions generally received strong support, although some groups of the migrant workers living in the hostels felt alienated, and also aggrieved, by the enforced boycott. Migrants living in hostels tended to be disconnected from the township, especially its politics. Most were unskilled workers who, in the absence of unions or legislative protection, could easily be replaced if they participated in what would have been deemed an illegal strike – and replacement would mean being forced back to the rural areas.

Tensions rose between hostel dwellers and township students. In September, migrant workers living at Mzimhlophe attacked township residents, with the support of the police, in one the darkest episodes of this period. Orlando West was one of the worst affected areas and it was no surprise, then, that students from this area, as well as from Meadowlands, organised retaliatory strikes against the hostel dwellers. Because of the serious disruptions to schooling and the continued detention of many colleagues, the SSRC called for a boycott of the end-of-year examinations. At Orlando High no student wrote the final matric examinations and the principal, Thamsanqa Khambule, who had occupied the post for two decades, resigned in protest against the state's actions. Five days after the uprising, older members of the community established the Black Parents Association to support the students. Winnie Mandela and Dr Nthatho Motlana were among the key figures in this new organisation.

In 1977 the state continued its attack on the anti-apartheid movement. On 12 September 1977 the leader of the Black Consciousness Movement, Steve Biko, was killed in detention. A month later, on 19 October, the state banned nineteen Black Consciousness organisations including the SSRC, Nayo, The Black People's Convention and Saso. Scores of activists were also rounded up in the early hours of the morning, which became known as 'Black Wednesday'. Student organisations were mostly unprepared for this scale of repression and many students temporarily withdrew from politics or went into hiding to avoid detention and harassment from the police. Many young people also decided to leave the country, often out of the real fear of being arrested, but mostly because they were convinced that the state's violence had to be countered by armed struggle. After the crackdown in 1976, thousands of young people chose this route. Colin Nxumalo assisted a few young men from Orlando to go into exile in Swaziland.

> We took these children ... I took those kombis and organised one of my friends ... Kitso Makume and Jabu Mkhwanazi, he had a bus, and Kitso Makume used his cars, we were actually taking these children to

> the border gate. By then I was a manager of the musical group called Young Lovers so I took the instruments and placed them on top of the kombi and as if we were going to the show. Then when we come across road blocks, [I said] 'no, no, *die mense hulle sing*' and I was a traffic cop. As we were about to cross the border gate next to Swaziland, about a kilometre away from the border gate, the children will get off and we will go and wait for them at the other side, whilst they jumped the fence. We then took them to Kwa-Manzini. I think we did about three trips and then they were starting to suspect me.

His concerns about coming under police surveillance were entirely valid. These cross-border operations were generally undertaken on an *ad hoc* basis, with very little planning, and with limited experience of carrying out clandestine activities. In February 1977, Nxumalo's role as courier was brought to an abrupt end.

> ... the security arrived and they took me. They took me and my wife, my late wife. They took us and locked us up at Jabulani Police Station. After two days they released her. I was left at the police station, after a while then Makume came, he was also arrested. We stayed at Jabulani Police Station for four months [in] solitary confinement, it was known as Section 6 of the Terrorism Act ... After four months when we came back from Jabulani Police Station then they took us to different police stations to do our case. They took me to Bramley, then they took Mr Makume to Jeppe, and Jabu [Mkhwanazi] was taken from Pietermaritzburg to Meadowlands Police Station. We stayed another four months at the Fort.

This clampdown by the state against political activists was the worst since the early 1960s. However, it failed to break the mood of resistance that had been building up, especially among the youth, throughout the 1970s. Within two years of 'Black Wednesday', new organisations were launched to carry forward the struggle against apartheid.

■ ■ ■ ■ ■

CHAPTER NINE

THE MAKING OF A MIDDLE CLASS

A SURVEY CONDUCTED IN 2006/7 BY THE CENTRE FOR SOCIOLOGICAL Research found that two-thirds of Soweto's inhabitants described themselves as middle class. According to the research, residents of the township attach multiple meanings to the term middle class, associating it with a range of issues: with the ability to consume, with education, with employment, and with social mobility, as well as with being self-sufficient and responsible. It is a complex and fluid identity. Aspiring to be middle class is of course not new, especially not in Orlando where members of the educated elite were prominent among the first group of inhabitants in the 1940s. Historically, having an education and being respectable were key markers of an urban middle class or elite status. So, too, were having a house and professional employment.

These ideas permeated the settled urban African population for a long time. The white government, however, aimed to curtail the emergence of an African working class, at least until the late 1970s.

In his autobiography, *Long Walk To Freedom*, Nelson Mandela described the house he moved into at Number 8115 Orlando West, on the corner of Vilakazi and Ngakane Streets: 'The house itself was identical to hundreds of others built on postage-stamp-size plots on dirt roads. It had the same standard tin roof, the same cement floor, a narrow kitchen, and a bucket toilet at the back. Although there were street lamps outside we used paraffin lamps as the homes were not yet electrified. The bedroom was so small that a double bed took up almost the entire floor space.' Even though the house was 'the opposite of grand', Mandela was 'mightily proud' because it was his 'first true home'. This was a sentiment shared by many people who moved into Orlando's new houses in the 1940s. Having a house symbolised the right of African families to be in the city. Built according to specifications, such as the '51/6 design on 40m² plot', these municipal houses were not only monotonous but were intended to enforce uniformity among urban Africans, to limit social difference in the township. In fact, only a handful of relatively well-off families were allowed to own houses and even then on the basis of a thirty-year leasehold.

From the late 1950s, the apartheid government redirected it attention, away from urban township and towards investing in homelands. Two main consequences of this shift were felt in places like Soweto from the 1960s: first, in 1968 the government abolished the leasehold system, denying Africans the right to own property in urban areas; second, the lack of investment in townships meant that the provision of housing came to a halt. According to the book *A History of Black Housing in South Africa*, the shortage of housing in Soweto began to be felt in the 1970s and by the end of the decade about 173 000 people were without homes. Overcrowding was inevitable. In the first instance people used all the available space inside their homes to accommodate families – living rooms and kitchens were converted to bedrooms at night. In the 1980s there was a mushrooming of backyard dwelling and when the influx control system was finally buried in the mid-1980s people spilled over into open fields to establish squatter camps.

By the end of 1977 a stalemate had developed between the state and the township youth, and the government felt sufficiently confident to embark on a limited reform programme. In the aftermath of the 1976 student uprising, the government established the Riekert and Wiehahn commissions to investigate issues pertaining to the status of black labour and of the urban black population. The Riekert commission admitted that African townships were faced with a deep crisis caused in part by poor local administration, financial difficulties and a steady increase in the urban population, especially as migration from the rural areas began to pick up again from the mid-1970s. Several analysts have evaluated the situation. According to the academics Jeremy Seekings and Karen Jochelson, the financial crisis was probably the most urgent issue because of the need to tackle the rapidly growing demand for new housing. By the late 1970s, Paul Hendler has shown, it would cost in the region of R764 million to overcome the housing shortage in African townships. The state's response to this crisis exposed an intractable dilemma: following a global trend and constrained by the deepening economic crisis, the government deliberately retreated from its responsibility to construct public housing in the townships –

precisely at the point when the demand for such housing was growing. The introduction of the 99-year lease scheme was a belated admission of the permanence of Africans in the urban areas (and by implication also an admission of the failure of its previous policies), and it was an attempt to encourage home ownership in the townships. Finally, the government now actively promoted private home ownership by allowing private housing companies to build houses in the townships.

The political rationale underpinning this decision was the attempt to create an urban African middle class, which apartheid policies had tried to suppress during the previous two decades. Such a middle class, it was hoped, would act as a bulwark between the state and the increasingly restive urban working class. Orlando was identified as one of the main areas in Soweto for this kind of middle class development.

Something of the sort, but on a smaller scale, had happened earlier, with the creation of an area in Orlando West known as 'Koppies'. Thami Zitha's family was one of the first to move into this new neighbourhood.

> This area, when it began, it was called Koppies. But it was for rich people. They are the ones who gave it the name Koppies, because it was an Afrikaner name. Eh, we were the first tenants in this place. It was during the time the Afrikaners were creating the black middle class. Before then there were no stands that were sold – people got their houses from the government. No stands were sold so that you could build your own house. This was the beginning of this thing of private house system or bond houses, where you don't build your house, but you have to buy a bond house. It was one bedroom, a kitchen and a dining room. That was it. Those were the municipality's houses. A family of five had to live in that house. It meant me and my brothers had to wake up early in the morning before any visitor could come. It was that situation. My father thought that the yard was not big enough to extend the house. In fact the development of this place, Koppies, and the start of the location, did not take too long. It began with a few people in 1975 and we moved in 1976.

In the late 1970s, Shadrack Mutau moved his family to 'Beverley Hills', the new middle class section in the heart of Orlando West.

> Later on I got my house built in 1978, because, as you know, the contribution of 1976 students made it possible for us to get houses built under the 99-year lease. When I was working for IBM, it organised nineteen sites, and I was one of those fortunate to get a house in the famous Vilakazi Street. Some of my colleagues, like George

Manicured lawns in Orlando

Photograph by Sakhile Mthabela

> Mxcadana, Simon Ngakane, Joe Maroleng, Sam Pamla – they were all IBM personnel. Therefore, we are actually proud of that because in my street, between Ngakane and Bacela, there were only three houses when I came here in 1978 ... But, for instance, my house when I got it, it cost me fourteen thousand rands. It was a whole lot of money during those years ... And my salary didn't actually qualify me to own this house, but fortunately I had some savings which I added onto my bond.

Shadrack Mutau was prepared to pay this much for a new house even though similar houses in another new middle class suburb, Selection Park, were costing only R6 000, because ' ... there used to be a sewerage dam. I could have acquired a house in that area, but because of that I had some sinus problem, you know, and therefore I could not stand that smell.' Beverley Hills was also occupied by members of the township elite:

> A third house from mine up there, Number 6975, belonged to the Buthelezi family. Mr Buthelezi was a business person. He owns shops even today. Another third house to the east belonged to Dr Mathlare. Behind, at the corner, that house at Hlathi Street, on the left hand side, belongs to the Maseko family. The diagonal opposite of

Photograph by Sally Gaule

Home improvements: middle class housing became more visible from the 1980s

> Maseko there was Mr Ngwenya's house. He was a black health education person, working for the Johannesburg City Council. Behind Mr Ngwena's house, there was Mr Jafta's house. Jafta used to work at the superintendent's office.

These new suburbs introduced a visible class distinction in Orlando, and elsewhere, as the new houses were usually bigger and constructed differently from the conventional matchbox houses. As Mrs Sithole says, 'You could tell the difference, though. When you look at these houses they are totally different. You would assume that our place was for the peasants, you know. And those were like they were staying in the suburbs. Their houses are beautiful.'

Shadrack Mutau remembers that residents living in the old sections viewed people in the new suburbs with some suspicion.

> The people [on the other side] were a bit sceptical about us, because they felt, you know, we are strangers, we stay in beautiful houses. That was animosity in a way, or jealousy. The acceptance was not so good, you know. Some of them were afraid of us. Who are these people? And immediately after that, because IBM and CitiBank built flats, the unique ones [in Vilakazi Street] … they perceived us to be high profile people.

Mrs Sithole recalls an incident in which the friction over the different classes came to a head. 'I remember there was a funeral in one of the houses there at the "suburbs" or high class people, as we used to call it.' She laughs, and continues.

> There was a man who said, 'We are aware of this barrier between these two places. This is for the second time we attend a funeral in this area and people from that side do not attend or come to our houses. This is bad.' He was furious. You know what, I got offended because I was from the same area he was talking about. And I quickly called him to order in public. I told him to stop talking nonsense because on no one's face is it written where they came from. I might even not be the only one from the other side. I told him to keep quiet. He was so shocked.

Mrs Sithole's anecdote reveals the complex ways in which residents of Orlando, and across Soweto, negotiated their class status. On the one hand, there had been a growing awareness of social differentiation, made visible by people's homes, the cars they drove and the clothes they wore. On the

Source: Community Collection

Mr Ngema stands proudly beside his luxury vehicle

other hand, there are those who insist on a common township identity that transcends these distinctions and also speaks to a sense of Soweto's distinctiveness in relation to other townships. In the popular imagination this is due to Soweto's role in the liberation struggle and the fact that it is the largest township in the country. But it also has to do with a sense that Soweto is generally better off than other areas. This was borne out to some extent by the 2001 census which showed that residents of this sprawling township fared slightly better than other African people in terms of several indicators: a greater proportion of Sowetans had access to basic amenities such as piped water and flushing toilets. They were also more successful consumers, owning more fridges, televisions, radios and telephones than residents of other townships.

Another factor that has set Soweto apart from other major townships is its employment profile. In Ekurhuleni on the East Rand, for instance, most of the working population were employed in the manufacturing sector. While many Sowetans could similarly be described as blue-collar workers, the large retail and business sectors in the Johannesburg/Sandton areas have traditionally been important sources of employment for Sowetans. So, too, have the education and medical professions. As Johannesburg's industrial sector began to shrink in the 1970s, the city began to grow into the financial centre of the country. This process accelerated from the early

1990s and, with the deracialisation of the economy, more middle and high ranking jobs became available to black people. By the turn of the twenty-first century more than forty per cent of Soweto's working population were to be found in professional and white collar jobs. More than seventeen per cent defined themselves as managers, educators, health professionals and public sector officials. A further twenty-four per cent were employed as office clerks and in the sales and service sectors. Some of these trends were already present and visible in the 1980s, but the attention given to, and the celebration of, class differences were subsumed then into the more urgent political task of overthrowing apartheid.

■ ■ ■ ■ ■

CHAPTER TEN

MAKING A REVOLUTION

State repression, and the ensuing lull, gave the impression that the movement sparked by the student uprising had been quelled. However, the quiescence that followed the banning of organisations in 1977 represented a mere pause in the emergence of a formidable anti-apartheid movement. The events of 1976 politicised thousands of young people across the country who came to represent a new generation of committed activists that would constitute the backbone of the struggle.

Although Thami Zitha was still in primary school in 1976, and so was not directly involved in the struggles, the uprising had a major influence on his life. For him, as for many of his generation, the Soweto uprising was the critical moment of his political awakening.

> In my family they knew that I liked debating and questioning things. I used to challenge my grandmother on Christianity. My grandmother used to say, no, no, Thamsanqa, don't worry, *andilikholwa mara difuna madishona diyophumela ecaweni* [I'm not a Christian but when I die I want my funeral to be held in church]. *Ja*, that's it. I'm an African. At that time I didn't know much. But I had a problem, challenging white supremacy. How did they become superior? By then I started to learn that this is my country and it was colonised, and what, what ... and all those things. I started to make sense of the situation. Because I had learnt about Jan van Riebeeck at school and all that ... so I was trying to find a way.

Thami Zitha was one of a new layer of youth who were becoming committed to struggle, but were still desperately searching for political answers to their many questions about apartheid, past struggles and the way forward. They found some of the answers among an older generation of political activists, some of whom were stalwarts of the liberation movements and had been imprisoned in the major crackdown in the early 1960s. Joe Gqabi, for example, spent more than a decade on Robben Island and on his return to Soweto he began to educate young people and draw them into an ANC network. Thami Zitha's political mentor was Peter Raboroko, one of the leaders of the Pan African Congress, the PAC.

> At that time I was fourteen. But then I started hooking up with and knowing all the old-timers who talked politics most of the time ... There was this old-timer in Orlando, at eMzimhlophe, next to my grandmother's place. He did not have a church or a congregation. His focus was to bury those who did not belong to any church and those who did not want their funeral to be held in church ...Well, he was a family friend, in fact my grandmother's friend. He was talkative, so every time we met or when I passed his house he would call me or ask me something, either to go to the shops and get something for him or ask me to give him a hand, and at that time he would talk. By then people were secretive about their political activities and when you started probing with more questions it showed that you were interested.

After a while he realised that the old man was not an ordinary community pastor.

> Now I started to connect with the pastor only to find out that he was a political activist, *ja*, and an Africanist. He is a political activist and his brother is already in exile. He is one of the PAC leaders ... He was a pastor. He was Raboroko. That's how our relationship started. From Raboroko I learnt a lot ... Where we lived also lived one of the PAC's leaders. He's the one who introduced me to Zeph [Zephania Mothopeng]. That's how I started to get connected.

The resilience of the post-1976 movement, based so much on the élan of youthful activists, was reflected in the emergence, at the end of the 1970s, of a range of organisations that transformed the local political landscape. The state's banning of Black Consciousness student organisations failed to halt the emergence of vibrant and militant student movements. From the late 1970s, the anti-apartheid movement began to experience a revival on

Source: SAHA

Soweto uprising

three major fronts. First was the consolidation of the independent trade unions, which had been making incremental gains since the early 1970s; most significant was the launch of Fosatu, the Federation of South African Trade Unions, in 1979. Then, in that same year, Cosas, the Congress of South African Students, and the Azanian Students' Organisation were launched, both of which were to play pivotal roles in the upsurge in student struggles in the 1980s. Finally, civic organisations sprang up in townships across the country. Soweto played a prominent role, especially in the civic and in the student and youth struggles, during this period.

In Soweto, civic struggles were led by the Soweto Civic Association, known as the SCA. Shadrack Mutau has observed that, initially constituted out of the Committee of Ten, the SCA, in the 1980s, included the political activists Isaac Mogase, Tom Manthata and Phillip Matthews. In 1980-81 the SCA launched a campaign against the proposed rent increases and played a leading role in the boycott campaign against the black local authorities. From the late 1970s onwards, the many causes of the growing discontent in African townships coalesced into a massive township-based insurrection against apartheid. More and more people streamed into the urban areas and, in the absence of public housing programmes, squatter settlements mushroomed in almost every existing township. For example, the number of backyard shacks in Katlehong grew fourfold (from 8 000 to 34 000) in the short space of two years, and in Soweto the number of families living in shacks had increased to 23 000 by 1982.

The state acknowledged the severity of the predicament but refused to allocate the required financial resources to resolving the problem – its policies were underpinned by the principle that townships should become self-financing. This refusal to provide anywhere near adequate funding for township development was a root cause of the crisis that enveloped the townships in the early 1980s. Traditional sources of income in the townships, such as profits from beerhalls and services levies, had dried up in the 1970s, and the only potential source of income was through rent increases – rendered by endemic poverty as a highly unlikely source of sufficient revenue to cover the costs of development.

At the same time as acknowledging the financial crisis, the state introduced changes to the local administration of townships. The Black Local Authorities Act of 1982 established a new system of local government in townships, one with very limited powers except to raise revenue. Thus, the central government deliberately shifted the political responsibility for the financial squeeze on residents onto local conservative politicians. Councillors enjoyed little support in their communities as was evidenced from local elections, in which only eight per cent of adult residents, nationally, bothered to cast their ballots. In Soweto, the figure was less than ten per cent.

Soweto Civic Association and the Ad Hoc Poster Group, (Screen Training Project)

Soweto Civic Association mobilised boycott of Community Councils

Local civics, supported by students and also by trade unions, led the boycott campaign against the black local authorities, and the formation of the United Democratic Front in August 1983 created a national umbrella and lent some political coherence to these various local struggles. Soweto activists such as Albertina Sisulu and Winnie Mandela again played key roles in this new movement.

The insurrection of the 1980s reached a climax between 1984 and 1986. An absolutely pivotal period in this development was the uprising that occurred between September and November 1984, triggered by the decision of the Lekoa Town Council to increase rents by nearly R6 despite widespread protests from the community. In September, the Vaal Civic Association called a rent boycott and stayaway to pressurise the authorities to reverse the rent increases, but its action was met by violence from the police, including the shooting of protesters and large scale arrests of activists. Organisations in Soweto called a stayaway in solidarity with the Vaal communities, although this action enjoyed uneven support from the different parts of the township. In mid-October, Fosatu and Cosas joined forces to mobilise a regional strike. More than a million workers and students, mainly from Soweto, the Vaal and East Rand, heeded the call. After that, almost every township was engulfed by the anti-apartheid struggle.

Students and the youth were in the forefront of the township uprising. Shirley Thathi talks about her involvement in student politics during the 1980s.

> While I was doing Form Two I was a member of the SRC, and I was an active member. In 1976, I was around. I saw a bit, because I was only six years old. When we got out of school in Mzamo we would run, and we saw the teargas and stuff. And when we got home, we could hear when people were talking about it. I did not really understand much about 1976 as such, but I got the influence from my brother-in-law. So at Matshidiso [Secondary] I had that spirit. I was elected to the SRC, and I started being active then. Our principal was a *boer* and I learned to speak English through him, even though I was not perfect. He could understand me when I was cross or angry. We really fought for the students when I was doing Standard Eight.

According to Shirley's testimony, the main demands of students in Orlando echoed those of students across the country.

> It was against corporal punishment. Number two was that we should get free education and not pay fees and the like. Also, students to have a right to voice things that they did not like, and that teachers and students should address issues among themselves. Sometimes we were mediators as SRC. We would listen to both sides of the story and if one party was wrong, they should apologise to the other.

Other demands included an end to the prefect system, the introduction of parent teachers associations, the abolition of the age limit, and state investment to upgrade the quality of schools and education in general. Students demonstrated, and embarked on class boycotts to press home their demands. Shirley remembers an instance of the state's response: 'This was the time when they even sent soldiers to our school.'

> We were guarded by soldiers at school at some stage, where we were expected to go to the toilet only once and after a certain time. You could not go to the toilet [until] after thirty minutes. They did not understand that we would be pressed to go to the loo at times. There is one guy who they shot and killed. Apparently, Hendrick went to the toilet and left the class again after five or ten minutes, or so. And this *boer* asked him why he was going out again and he said he was going to the toilet and this *boer* got angry and went to the hippo [armoured vehicle] and he shouted to another *boer* to move out of the

> way because he was going to shoot this boy. We were always under the impression that they were shooting with rubber bullets, but he shot him to death with a real bullet.

Under the circumstances, violent confrontations between the state security forces and the youth escalated from the mid-1980s, leading to deaths and injuries. The state also introduced emergency regulations, detained hundreds of young people and, in 1985, banned Cosas. Large scale arrests left a political vacuum of leadership in local organisations, especially among students and the youth, causing the onset of some disorganisation and political fragmentation. One manifestation of this was the emergence of what has been called the *comtsotsi* phenomenon. Shirley Thathi locates the origins of *comtsotsi's* at her school in a lack of discipline and deliberate misinterpretation of political positions:

> Yes, there were those whom we referred to as *comtsotsis,* where people would do things at school like getting out of the class just because he is not on good terms with the teacher. That was wrong because he did not do his work and we would tell them to go back to class.

But the activities and problems associated with *comtsotsis* extended beyond ill-discipline in the schools. And the intense conflict between state and activists, which assumed an increasingly militaristic character, plus questionable tactics employed by the youth movements to enforce boycotts, created spaces for the flourishing of *comtsotsi* behaviour. Shirley Thathi offers a valuable insight into how *comtsotsis* were associated with what she believes to be legitimate forms of struggle.

> Yes, *comtsotsi* was there but we were using the word 'target' because we were comrades … there were cars that used to come and do deliveries in the townships. Our concept was to destroy the economy of South Africa and that was the time when we were really oppressed in the country. So when we saw cars from the shops like OK, we would say, here is the target, and burn them, and take things … Our aim was not to take things in the car but to burn the white man's car. The *comtsotsis* wanted to take things from the car and take them home.

The violent enforcement of consumer boycotts by young comrades was increasingly associated with the activities of *comtsotsis.*

> By the time we wanted to call the consumer boycott, it was when we called the shop owners and asking them to drop prices so that

Photograph by Paul Weinberg. Courtesy Wits Historical Papers

ANC rally in Soweto

> they will get more customers. So we would inform all the parents about that and even send flyers all over. But there were those parents who would say, we are not going there, so it became painful when we asked those people to drink oil and even throw away stuff they bought. We would throw away groceries in the station and the *comtsotsis* would steal some groceries and take them home. We did not want those things to be taken by someone but [it was] to show those parents who did not understand, to see what it was like when we say we must boycott.

One of the main reasons behind the decline in gangsterism and crime in Soweto from the mid-1970s was that many youths, who previously were drawn into gangs, became involved in political activism. Youth and student organisations also campaigned against crime and, over time, they developed sufficient political authority to marginalise and discipline the gangs. In the late 1980s, therefore, the temporary decline of political organisations created opportunities for the re-emergence of gangsterism. In Soweto the most notorious were the jackroller gangs. Mbulelo Mbehle has described the particular forms of violence associated with this group.

> Yes, they had weapons, they were full of shit, full of shit, they were terrorists, they took women by force. No, they said it's to *rutla*, take women by force, they were jackrollers. When they got to the stokvel they took women by force. They had families … but they were rapists, people knew that when they were in the house anything could happen … some had gone to school ... they drank and drank, when they got out there, you find that they were involved with robbery somewhere in town. Now they are busy with women, sometimes they don't even ask women nicely. Sometimes you find that women run when they see them, they will jump the fence and they will hunt her down until they find her, they will make sure that she sits next to them. This jackroll stuff, hey, those guys were feared.

The question of youth and violence during the struggle against apartheid has been a source of contention. The government pointed to this violence to argue that the struggle was anarchic. A sensitive and critical study of 'young warriors' in the Diepkloof area of Soweto, by the sociologist Monique Marks argued that a distinction had to be drawn between the criminality of groups such as the jackrollers and political violence which could not be ascribed to lawlessness but was driven by the over-arching aim of overthrowing apartheid. One of the many factors contributing to the increase in youthful violence during this period was the difficulty township-based organisations experienced through state repression, especially the detention of many key leaders. But things began to change in the late 1980s.

State repression failed to break the insurrectionary movement, and by late 1988 anti-apartheid struggles regained momentum. This was largely due to the campaigns led by the trade union movement, especially the Congress of South African Trade Unions, Cosatu, from its launch in December 1985. In 1989, many civic organisations were revived. A defiance campaign was launched which signalled the start of a new wave of township-based popular struggles, prompting the government to begin a process of engaging the leaders of the liberation movements and to embark on the road of negotiations towards a programme of reform. In October 1989, several leaders of the ANC and PAC were released from imprisonment on Robben Island. Among them was Walter Sisulu whose arrival back home in Orlando West sparked massive celebrations. Four months later his old comrade Nelson Mandela was also released, and returned to his home in Vilakazi Street. Tens of thousands of people filled the streets of Soweto to welcome home the leaders of the liberation movement.

It was also a moment that inaugurated formal negotiations for a new South Africa. At a local level, the Soweto Civic Association had already spearheaded a campaign from the late 1980s to transform the relationship between Soweto and Johannesburg. It campaigned for the integration of Soweto and Johannesburg into a single urban administration, captured in the slogan, 'One City, One Tax Base'. Sowetans, the civics argued, were contributing enormously through their labour, spending power and taxation to the development of the city, but remained marginalised and underdeveloped. Spurred on by the political changes in 1990, the Johannesburg authorities signed the Soweto Accord with the civics, which saw the formation of the Central Witwatersrand Metropolitan Chamber, charged with the responsibility of negotiating an end to the apartheid city and the creation of a united city. The promise of 'a better life for all' seemed finally within reach.

Change, however, happened slowly for most Sowetans. According to the census of 2001, Soweto's population stood at 1,1 million, about forty-three per cent of Johannesburg's population. The same census showed that fifty-eight per cent of households lived in brick houses, the vast majority of them former council houses. However, a survey conducted in the late 1990s by sociologists at the University of the Witwatersrand found that there were approximately 121 000 backyard shacks in Soweto, about the same number as formal houses. A further 18 000 shacks were squeezed into twenty-seven squatter settlements spread across the township (although many people in Orlando West also erected backyard dwellings to accommodate relatives and newcomers, the area did not experience as much squatting

Photograph by Sally Gaule

Photograph by Sally Gaule

ABOVE: Informal economy in Soweto

LEFT: New RDP housing developing

as some other parts of the township). Soweto also suffers from high levels of unemployment (forty per cent according to the 2001 census) and has experienced a massive growth in the informal sector.

In 2004 the Johannesburg City Council began to move residents from squatter settlements to new housing complexes such as Braamfischerville to the west of Soweto. The City Council has also targeted specific areas in Soweto for development, including Kliptown, the area around Chris Hani Baragwanath Hospital and the Vilakazi Street precinct, a project that is converting an area that includes the Hector Pieterson Museum, the Mandela House Museum, the Tutu family home, Uncle Tom's Hall and Vilakazi Street into an integrated development and heritage zone. One of the objectives of the project is to celebrate the rich and diverse history of the people of Orlando West.

■ ■ ■ ■ ■

SELECTED REFERENCES

Beall J, O Crankshaw and S Parnell (2002) *Uniting a Divided City: Governance and Social Exclusion in Johannesburg.* London: Earthscan.

Beavon K (2004) *Johannesburg. The Making and Shaping of the City.* Pretoria: Unisa Press.

Bonner P and L Segal (1999) *Soweto – A History.* Cape Town: Maskew Miller Longman.

Bonner P and N Nieftagodien (2001) *Kathorus – A History.* Cape Town: Maskew Miller Longman.

Bonner P and N Nieftagodien (2008) *Alexandra – A History.* Johannesburg: Wits University Press.

Ndlovu S (2004) 'The Soweto Uprising', *The Road to Democracy in South Africa, 1970-1980.* Pretoria: Sadet.

French K (1983) 'James Mpanza and the Sofasonke Party in the Development of Local Politics in Soweto'. MA Thesis, University of the Witwatersrand.

Glaser C (2000) *Bo-Tsotsi: The Youth Gangs of Soweto, 1935-1976.* Cape Town: David Philip.

Hendler P (1989) *Politics on the Home Front,* Johannesburg: South African Institute of Race Relations.

Hindson D (1988) *Pass Controls and the Urban African Proletariat in South Africa.* Braamfontein: Ravan.

Hirson B (1989) *Yours for the Union: Class and Community Struggles in South Africa, 1930-1947.* Johannesburg: Wits University Press.

Lodge T (1983) *Black Politics in South Africa Since 1945.* Johannesburg: Ravan.

Mandela W (1985) *Part of My Soul Went With Him.* New York, WW Norton.

Marks M (2001) *Young Warriors: Youth Politics, Identity and Violence in South Africa.* Johannesburg: Wits University Press.

Morris P (1980) *A History of Black Housing in South Africa.* Johannesburg: South African Foundation.

Phadi M and C Ceruti (2011) 'Multiple meanings of the middle class in Soweto, South Africa'. *African Sociological Review* 15(1).

Phillips H (2011) 'Locating the location of a South African Location: The Paradoxical Pre-history of Soweto', paper presented at, Shadow Cities Conference, University of London, June 2011.

Posel D (1991) *The Making of Apartheid, 1948-1961: Conflict and Compromise.* Oxford: Clarendon Press.

Segal L and P Holden (2008) *Great Lives: Pivotal Moments.* Johannesburg: Jacana Media.

Sisulu E (2003) *Walter and Albertina Sisulu. In our lifetime.* Cape Town: David Philip.

Stadler A (1979) 'Birds in the Cornfield: Squatter Movements in Johannesburg, 1944-1947'. *Journal of Southern African Studies,* 6,1.

CHAPTER ELEVEN

PHOTOGRAPHIC ESSAY

INTRODUCTION

The homes of Walter Sisulu, Bishop Desmond Tutu and former President Nelson Mandela are celebrated in this historic suburb, and the 1976 Soweto uprising is very much present in the memories of residents and visitors alike. But not much is known about the day to day lives of those who live there today.

The streets of Orlando West show the imprint of time. The houses modelled on the NE 51/9 (matchbox) design were the characteristic form that emerged on the South African landscape as apartheid got underway. In some photographs, the original houses built in the 1940s and 50s – or thereabouts – survive, virtually unchanged in all this time, while others have been renovated and altered; their facades are an image of the ways in which Soweto and the residents themselves have changed over time. Photography, as Bronwyn Law-Viljoen reminds us, 'is a marker of change, a maker, in profoundly ambiguous ways, of history'.

During the course of the project we documented this changing landscape. Together with Sakhile Mthebela (himself a resident of neighbouring Mzimhlope, and the best of photographic companions), my *modus operandi* was to walk the streets and speak to the residents, who frequently invited us inside their houses. Not many photographers have this opportunity, which makes real its people and testifies to the generosity of Orlando West residents.

Many of the houses here have been passed down from generation to generation: the Theku family on the corner of Vilakazi and Khuele streets are renovating their house to accommodate their extended family; Mrs Dominica Nomsa Modirapula, and Mrs Neo Masike have lived in their houses for decades; and the Ndlovu family have lived in their house since 1949. This is a place called home. In the suburbs of Johannesburg we hardly know our neighbours. We rarely talk to them. Instead we greet them from our motor cars when we pass by. Here people *walked*, and they greeted each other. Significantly, what remains here is the life of the street, a feature that is strikingly absent in the walled suburbs of Johannesburg.

One rainy misty day we came across a beautiful garden next to a kopje where David Tlale and his wife Bella live. He loves gardening and has singlehandedly created a sanctuary, green lawn, dahlias and roses, made entirely with his own money and by his own efforts. The next time we visited it was 42°C, yet Mr Tlale welcomed us, and spent an hour standing in the sun explaining what he still hoped to do in his garden.

When we talked to Dumisane Hlubi, who has been trading outside the Hector Pieterson Museum since 2001, he said that we were blessed to host the world cup. 'I don't think we will get the opportunity again, because lots of countries want to host it. Maybe next century. Sometimes [trading] is good, sometimes not, but you have to accept it. In this job I've met many people, Sepp Blatter, Nelson Mandela, even Bill Clinton'.

On another occasion we visited the former women's hostel in Orlando, where the units have been renovated into family accommodation. A group of friends was visiting from elsewhere in Soweto, relaxing in the shade outside one of the houses (these houses measure less than 42m^2, and so there is no space to sit inside). With the same generosity of spirit, we talked and were given food, and it was here that I had my first sip of *mqombothi*.

Photographs don't show a before or an after. Rather they depict a moment extracted from the continuum of time. They are also episodic and fragmentary and, because of these limitations, offer only glimpses of life, a fraction of experience. Accordingly, these photographs show only a tiny proportion of the richness of life in Orlando West.

Sally Gaule

May, 2012

Interior of former President Mandela's home

Mandela House
8115 Vilikazi Street

Mrs Neo Masike
23 Khuele Street, Orlando West

HALALA

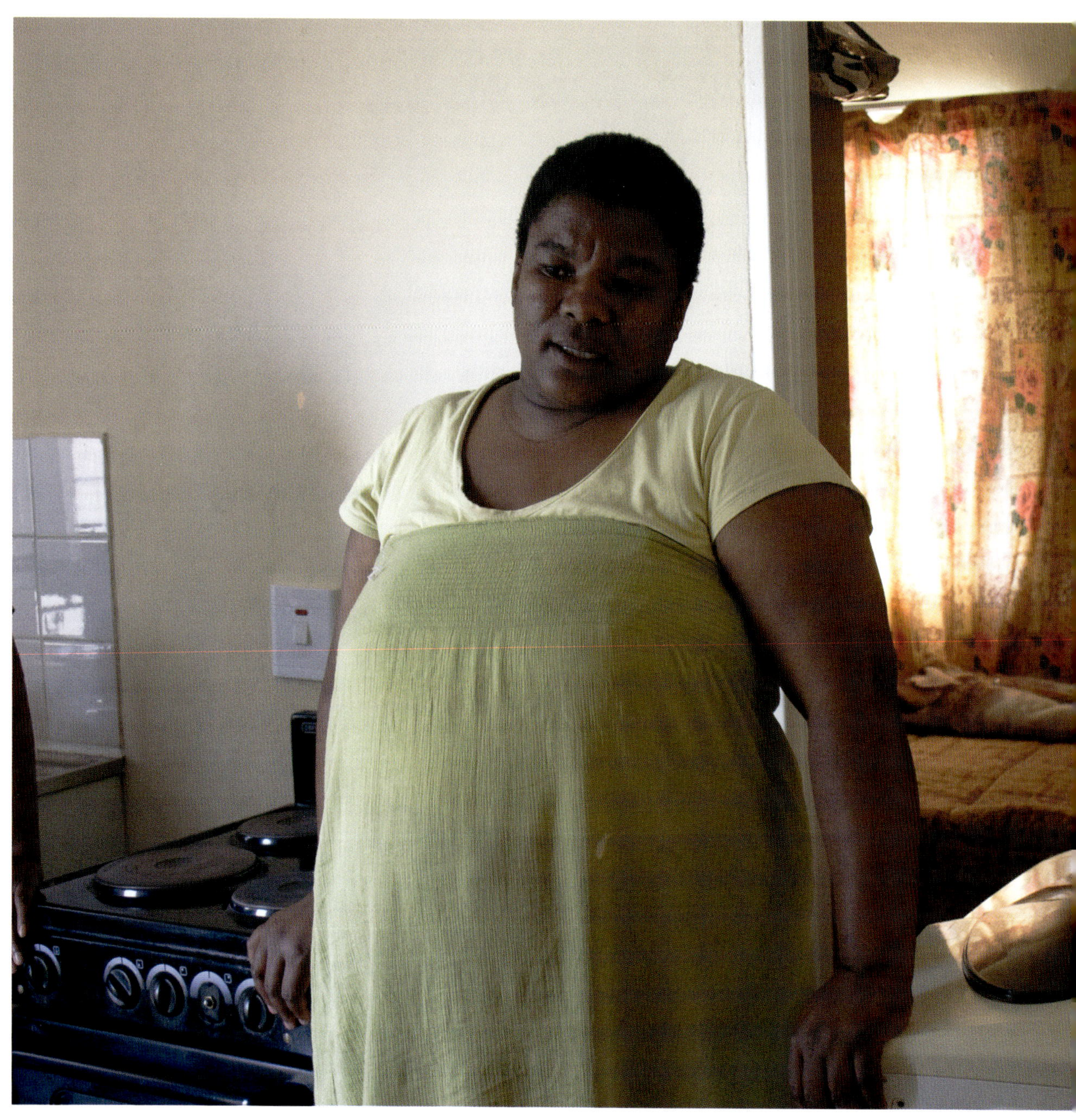

Nombulelo Khesa visiting her friend Agnes Kelebogile Andries
125B, Orlando West

Mrs Dominica Nomsa Modirapula
7080 Khuele Street, Orlando West

8257

CARLING Black Label BEER
FRIENDS IN PROGRESS
LIQUOR STORE
Coca-Cola
Friends in Progress
Liquor Store

Mandela House, 8115 Vilikazi Street

THE CENTREPOINT OF MY WORLD ... ANY HOUSE

SCHNITZER

Khumalo Street, Orlando West

Former women's Hostel, Orlando West

EVE

THE SHOOTING OF HECTOR PIETERSON
VILAKAZI STREET PRECINCT

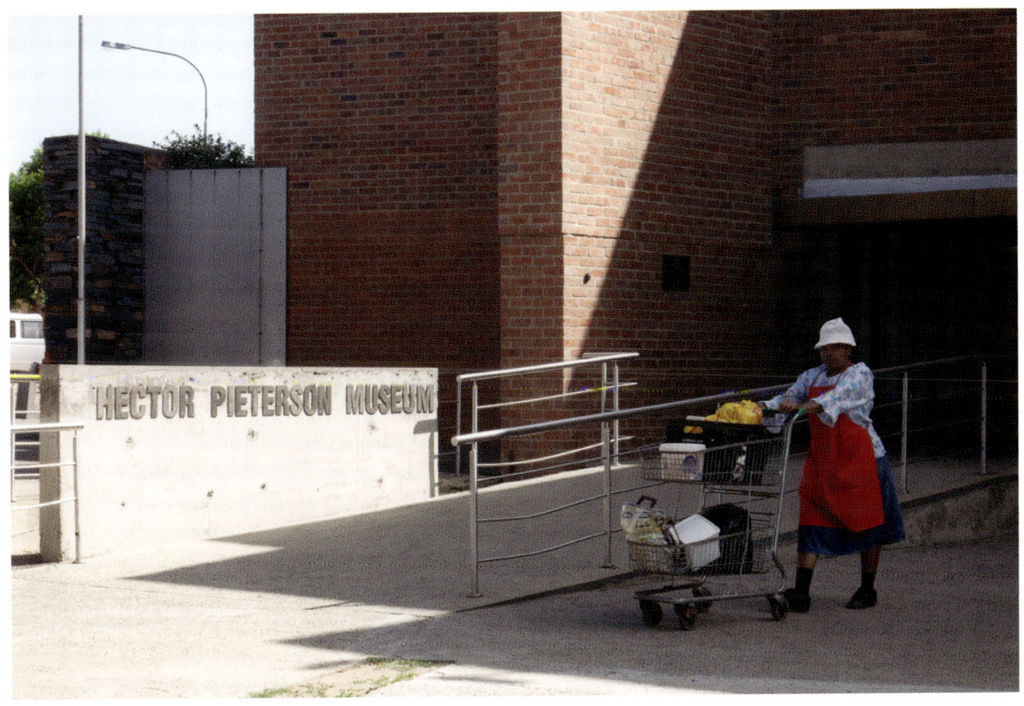
HECTOR PIETERSON MUSEUM

Anita (left) and Mfuno (right) selling chicken heads and chicken feet ('Mawotwa'), the price of which they say is '8 bob'

POLAR
Ice Cream

ORLANDO

Anna, Moema Street, Orlando West

9070

JOKO
GIVES YOU STRENGTH
JOKO
MTN
JOKO

Khumalo Street

Thando Modirapula
7080 Khuele Street, Orlando West

Vilikazi Street (left) and Ms Seipati Modirapula (right) 7080 Khuele Street, Orlando West

Checking matric results in Moema Street

Playing Monopoly in Maseko Street, Orlando West

Vilikazi Street

Traders outside Hector Pieterson Museum

ORLANDO WEST
CHIPBOARDS

Khumalo Street, Orlando West

Mr and Mrs Ndlovu
7245 Vilakazi Street, Orlando West

Agnes Kelebogile, 125B Orlando West

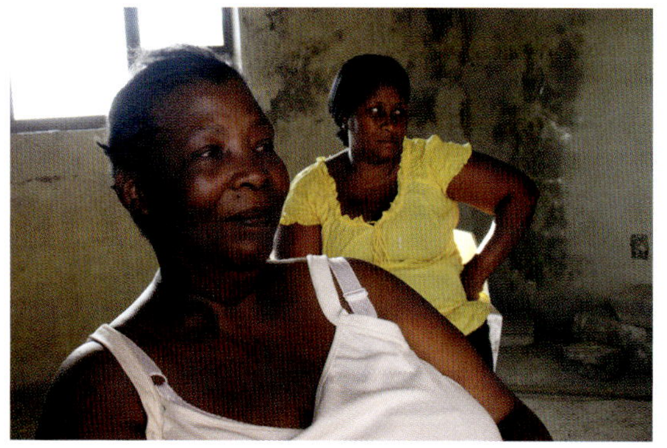

Mrs Thandi Theku

Mr Dumisani Hlubi

Chiefs supporter

Boitumelo Zulu, Bonolo Moloi and Kamogelo Rapoo (back) in Khulele Street

Mr Ndlovu
Vilikazi Street

Siphokazi Ngecphe
23 Khuele Street

Khuele Street

ANC

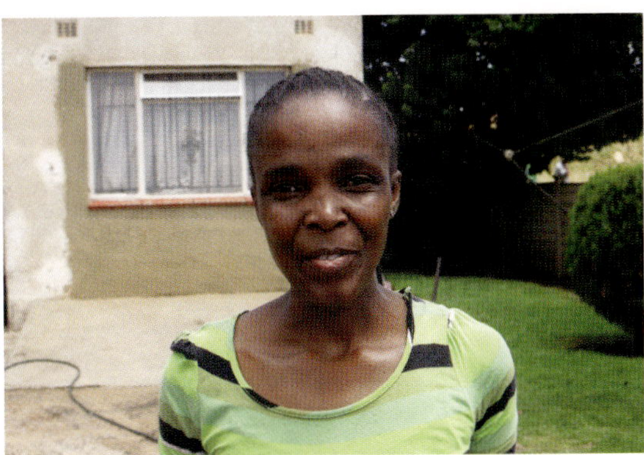

MASEKO

David Tlale in his garden, Orlando West

The Best Love
The Best Love